# Hello new Life

A Christian Guide for Finding
Hope, Healing, and Happiness after Divorce

## Paula Nilsen

For more information, visit paulanilsen.com or
email info@paulanilsen.com

Published in the United States by Avant Publications, LLC. Grand Forks, North Dakota.

Library of Congress Control Number: 2018901285

ISBN-13: 978-1983789717
ISBN-10: 1983789712

Scripture quotations from the English Standard Version (ESV) unless otherwise identified.

Scripture taken from the Amplified Bible. Copyright © 1954, 1958, 1962. 1964. 1965, 1987 by The Lockman Foundation. Used by permission.

"Scripture quotations are from the ESV® Bible (The Holy Bible, English Standard Version®), copyright © 2001 by Crossway, a publishing ministry of Good News Publishers. Used by permission. All rights reserved."

Scripture quotations marked MSG are taken from THE MESSAGE, copyright © 1993, 1994, 1995, 1996, 2000, 2001. 2002 by Eugene H. Peterson. Used by permission of NavPress. All rights reserved. Represented by Tyndale House Publishers. Inc.

Scriptures taken from the Holy Bible. New International Version®, NIV®. Copyright © 1973, 1978, 1984, 2011 by Biblica, Inc.™ Used by permission of Zondervan. All rights reserved worldwide. www.zondervan.com The "NIV" and "New International Version" are trademarks registered in the United States Patent and Trademark Office by Biblica, Inc.™

Scripture taken from the New King James Version®. Copyright © 1982 by Thomas Nelson. Used by permission. All rights reserved.

Scripture quotations marked (NLT) are taken from the Holy Bible, New Living Translation, copyright ©1996, 2004, 2007, 2013, 2015 by Tyndale House Foundation. Used by permission of Tyndale House Publishers. Inc., Carol Stream, Illinois 60188. All rights reserved.

Cover design by Carissa Odegaard.

To my niece:
Because she loves my writing, it is to her then that I write.

# From the Author

*Hello New Life* is the story of finding hope, healing, and happiness after divorce. If you are on this path, I wish to share my thoughts with you. The reality about our current circumstances, whether we've created the mess ourselves, someone else led us into the darkness, or somewhere in between, is that we have a unique ability to change our reactions to those circumstances and remake our lives.

I rarely make New Year's resolutions. My resolutions invariably come to me at the completion of a beautiful book or discussing a new idea. I am most successful when I allow my old, stagnant thoughts to be replaced with new and beautiful ideas. The paradox of letting go in order to receive staggers the mind. A New Year's Eve tradition in southern Italy speaks of letting go to make room for something new. Custom dictates that individuals part with an item, usually a possession. These old items are tossed out the window, and the last day of the year is one of decluttering and releasing. Ergo, the first day of the New Year becomes the day with some freed-up space for that new end table, bookcase, or trinket. Certainly, it must feel good to get rid of old, unwanted things. It sounds easy in terms of possessions, but in terms of releasing crippling memories and bad moods that have taken root, this is an entirely different story.

In the Gospel of Mark, the rich, young ruler came to Jesus and asked what he must do to inherit eternal life. He measured his life using the Ten Commandments and determined that he was already a good person. Yet his question to Jesus suggests that something was amiss. Jesus lovingly told him that one thing remained for him to do—an action was required. Since he could not do that one thing, he went away sorrowful (Mark 10:17-27). He chose business as usual over transformation.

Something will always be amiss when we refuse to release that "one thing." However, it is possible to walk away joyful and refreshed unlike the rich, young ruler. I know this from experience. I had to release that "one thing" many times. I wish you well in your daily endeavors of releasing as you move forward. As you read *Hello New Life,* may you gain insight, find healing, and make some "new you" resolutions. I invite you in.

Blessings,
Paula

# 1

# Hello Old Life

Everything was going so different from what I had allowed for.
Huck Finn, *The Adventures of Huckleberry Finn*

I recall our last day together. There we sat, facing the judge and the court reporter. The courtroom deputy sheriff sat on the sidelines, ready should things turn nasty. I wanted to dismiss him, to tell him that his services were not needed, that this had been a union created in love. He stayed; his gun ready at a moment's notice.

My husband was sitting on one side of the courtroom, me on the other; there were two lawyers separating us, each taking the aisle seat. Ours had not been a violent union. We didn't need to be separated like two brawling eight-year-old children. Nevertheless, we followed protocol.

There were no spectators present like the day we joined the union. We had more days to plan for the court hearing than we did for the wedding. I made a great effort to compose myself with dignity. I felt exposed, overwhelmed, and overpowered with a sense of hopelessness. My twenty-year marriage had ended, and the judge was left to sort through twenty years of history to determine our fate.

When I started to write this book, it had been over a year since that memory. Everything had long been finalized, yet within, little was. I hadn't moved forward; I hadn't healed.

### Coming Face-to-Face with Grief

Grief, I learned, has many layers. It is constant, exhausting, repetitive, and troubling. I needed to grieve my loss, not yearn for my old life. The intense longing came when I looked back to my old life, remembering only the perfect: my beautiful house in order; dinner in the oven. I could be found on the porch with an espresso in hand, the husband—not the one seated in the court-appointed seat but the one who loved me—arriving home and kissing me. And just like that, the mirage was gone.

> I needed to grieve my loss, not yearn for my old life.

My heart rejoiced momentarily but was quickly crushed under the weight of its deception. It was near enough that I felt the presence of my former self. Her nearness was eerie yet comforting. It was comforting in the way that I knew her well; I knew her better than the new person I'd become. It was eerie because it wasn't me anymore. The mirage for me was an oasis in my dry desert; it was a momentary lapse of reality. But the reality was this: there were no springs in the desert. It was an unwelcoming, angry desert and nightfall was upon me. I was parched, and at every turn, my wounded spirit became more wounded. The realization sunk in; I'd never have that life back.

What would I do with the nostalgia of winter that turned into spring that turned into summer that turned into fall that turned into Thanksgiving that turned into Christmas? All of the firsts brought with them their own waves of emotion. I suffered many times thinking about the holidays; then I suffered again on those days when they occurred. C.S. Lewis in *A Grief Observed* compared his suffering to a toothache. "I lay awake all night with a toothache, thinking about [the] toothache, and about lying awake. Part of every misery is, so to speak, the misery's shadow or reflection: the fact that you don't merely suffer but have to keep on thinking about the fact that you suffer." I had to make peace with my suffering.

Dear friend, I broke free from the pain, but it did not happen overnight. It happened over a five-year period. In a grief class, I was told to plan one year of healing for every four years of marriage. This advice allowed me to give myself a break. If I needed five years to heal, then I would allow for that. But here's the thing: I didn't understand grief. This was my first time coming face to face with constant grief. I quickly learned that grief would be present with me for the long haul; it was heavy, something I wanted to shed. I wanted to feel good again, to be delighted with life and be happy, effective immediately. But that was not the way of grief. The way of grief required long-suffering.

So I gave my grief human qualities and asked who she was. She said, "Primarily, I am love. With certainty, I am wise. I am but a thought—sometimes many thoughts. Whatever you do, do not set them aside. Muse over them. Stay open to me. Don't digress. Stay on topic. Lastly, think of me as your pilot fish. Let me explain." And she did, as only grief knows how. It was my voice she used.

My pain had attached itself to me like a pilot fish attaches itself to a shark, feeding off its prey and living on its host. My grief, ever present—my pilot fish—rendered me inept. Heartache and sadness took over my life and filled me with fear. It was C.S. Lewis who said in his book on grief, "No one ever told me that grief felt so much like fear." My fear was this: how could I possibly live without him? He had been there, and by "there," I mean, present for twenty years of my life.   He knew me better than anyone else and I, him. I missed his presence so much that his absence was intolerable. I missed his voice. I missed his friendship. I missed calling him at work to find out when he'd be home for supper. What would I do with the phone numbers I had memorized, both his cell phone and work number? They were on speed dial; deleting them was akin to deleting him. I missed hearing the garage door open at night, the sound of the door opening, with a sigh of relief, "Ah! He was home." Friday nights became unbearable and lonely. I was accustomed to

**I had experienced a death, yet we both lived.**

him, like I am to my own breath. I had experienced a death, yet we both lived. My breathing became shallow; I had to remind myself to breathe.

As time went by, the healthy part of me that was strong and bold and shark-like had frittered away. I only had the characteristics of the pilot fish, clingy and adhering, entering into my new life, floundering and insecure. The pilot fish takes its nutrients from the shark, ridding it of parasites, cleaning its teeth. In return, the shark doesn't eat this small fish but offers protection—both benefit from the agreement. I wasn't benefitting at all from my shark. In fact, the healthy side of me became like the pilot fish, taking on its characteristics: needy and unable to fend for myself. My whole person was grieving. I must allow my grief—a natural emotion—do what it was designed to do. I needed to live with the loss and learn to be healthy emotionally.

There's one last thing about sharks that fits so well here. When a shark is captured and hoisted onto a boat, pilot fish have been known to swim alongside the boat all the way back to the shore as a way to stay close to their host. The boat becomes the new host. At some point, the pilot fish must separate from the boat to survive. The current reality for me was this: he was gone, but I pursued him in my heart. I was like the pilot fish that clung to the boat that offered no life, no sustenance.

I wanted to survive. I wanted to live, to *really* live. First, I needed to make peace with the old life and learn to embrace the new life.

My difficulty came when I met my old life. Grief hung over me like a cloud: at Walmart, at the library, at church, in the sound of a bread maker, on the porch, and even with family. One day, as I was running errands, beside myself with emotion, I thought, *Do I have to pull this vehicle over again just to cry?* The truth was I had little control over my emotions; my grief had rendered me incapable of performing mundane tasks.

This is how I embraced my pilot fish of grief: I spoke to my old life. I adopted the saying, "Hello old life." Then I welcomed the old. I would stay in that moment for as long as I needed to grieve. It was necessary that I acknowledge each loss as it came and spend that moment in quiet reflection. If I was driving, I'd pull over for a time of reflection; if I was in Walmart, I'd find a quiet place to honor the old life, grieve its loss. It was never pretty! This very action is what helped me to begin the next phase of my life.

> I adopted the saying, "Hello old life."

After grieving, I'd say, "Goodbye old life, until next time." Sometimes, the next time was five minutes later. With each thought came the same greeting and the same sending away, similar to what I learned in Lamaze classes. During labor, I welcomed each contraction with a deep breath, endured the pain as long as it lasted, then I would exhale it away. I was thankful for a moment of reprieve; it gave me time to prepare for the next onslaught of pain, each pain worse than the last.

I found strength and comfort with this exercise during the process of severing myself from my husband. I could not allow my thoughts to steal my joy forever. I must "feel them, heal them, and then move on," according to Susan Elliott in *Getting Past Your Breakup*. I became thankful for the moments of reprieve. With this exercise, the moments of reprieve lengthened, and the moments of despair and grief lessened. Unlike labor that worsened with each contraction, the pain from divorce became easier to endure as time went by. Each month seemed a little easier, each year, more joyful. My pilot fish of grief had separated itself from the boat; it wanted to live.

Grief spoke to me once again, but it could very well have been the voice of God: "Adjust. Stretch where you need to stretch." I had begun to do just that. Glimpses of happiness came with each adjustment I made as I allowed for adversity. In times of adversity, it is my grandmother's voice I hear: "There are always adjustments in life." Another elderly lady, unknown to me, gave me a glimmer of hope and happiness when I read her story. She was 92 years old and moving into a nursing home. Upon arriving at her "new" home, the attendant described her room to her. Her response was, "I love it." The attendant was shocked at her enthusiasm for she hadn't yet seen it. The elderly lady replied, "That doesn't have anything to do with it. Happiness is something you decide on ahead of time. How I like my room doesn't depend on how the furniture is arranged; it's how I arrange my mind." Happiness is all about perspective.

Norman Vincent Peale in *The Power of Positive Thinking* shares the words of Dr. Karl Menninger: "Attitudes are more important than facts." Peale recommends repeating those words "until truth grips you," and he warns, "How you think about a fact may defeat you before you ever do anything about it." Moving forward would require some rearranging in my mind.

**Happiness is all about perspective.**

### Coaching Corner

Dear Fellow Pilot Fish,

My hope for you is that you learn to be present with your grief. Whispering the words *hello old life* helped me to recognize these moments for what they were—the past calling. Do this: roll out the red carpet to welcome those memories, repeat *hello old life, hello old life, hello old life*. Do whatever you need to do to recognize the siren call of your old life. These enchanting voices of the past will lure you into their clutches. If you steer your ship in their direction, you'll shipwreck. Understand that it is not the voice of the present; it is not how things are now. Understand that the old life is messing with you, messing with your happiness, messing with your ability to move forward.

When you finish grieving, send those thoughts packing with a resounding, *goodbye old life.* Try this simple exercise as often as necessary.

In classical Greek mythology, there is a river in Hades where all who drink from it immediately forget their past. Although this sounds wonderful, we have no such elixir. I urge you to turn to God. He understands suffering. You are made in His image, in His likeness. You are *imago Dei*, a Latin term that defines humanity's relationship to God (Genesis 1:27).

What does your life look like through His eyes?

### *Prayer*

*Jesus, I am made in Your image. Help me to look like You, to act like You, to forgive like You. Let me see my obstacles through Your eyes. I have Your God-like qualities within. Allow me to draw on those qualities as I heal from divorce. Let me see Your miraculous power that resides inside of me. The Bible tells us "the one who endures to the end shall be saved" (Matthew 24:13). Enduring suggests difficulty. That is where I find myself right now. I pray that I can see myself how You see me. I am the spitting image of You. I am imago Dei. I hang on to the promise that "when [I] pass through the waters, [You] will be with [me]; and through the rivers, they shall not overflow [me]" (Isaiah 43:2). Jesus, I place my trust in You.*

## Your Turn

❧ What's another way of looking at your situation? How about looking at it through God's eyes? What might that mean?

❧ When the past calls out to you, how are you prepared to handle it?

❧ What resources do you have available to overcome the adversities you will face while going through divorce?

❧ What is your greatest hindrance?

❧ What are the steps you might take today to ensure happiness tomorrow?

❧ Nobody ever teaches us how to fall out of love. How can you do this?

❧ Humanity has an amazing ability to adapt. How adaptable are you?

❧ How can you begin to think like the person you want to become?

# 2

# When Nostalgia Speaks

"I could tell you my adventures—beginning from this morning," said Alice a little timidly; "but it's no use going back to yesterday because I was a different person then."

Lewis Carroll, *Alice in Wonderland and Through the Looking Glass*

The revolving door won't budge. I push with all my might. Then I see her. She is pushing with all her might too, in the opposite direction, toward me. We struggle. I lose my footing. She gains ground. Then I gain my footing once again, pushing her backward. It is the "one step forward, two steps back" kind of dance with neither advancing.

That person in the partition just ahead of me stops. Her hands on the glass panel in front of me are similar to my own. She looks me straight in the face—she looks just like me. The gravity of the situation is this: I can't move forward to the new life; she can't go back to the old. I am blocking her, and she is blocking me. I will never be victorious if I persevere in this manner.

What is this thing standing in my way? Who is she? What is she? And then she speaks:

I am Nostalgia. *Ah yes, name your emotions.*

In Nostalgia's hand is a book. The title reads *The Life of Paula*. It's opened to today's date, but as she is never satisfied with today, she impetuously flips backward. She goes back, way back to my formative years when I was a missionary kid living in Stockholm. She knows my intense longing for my other home during the Christmas season. She's perceptive. I'll give her that.

Along with being perceptive, Nostalgia is also deceptive, with her partial truths showing only the good, leaving me hungry for that *other* life. She shows me the cozy Christmases of long ago with advent candles and brightly lit stars in the windows that shed light on a dark, snowy December day. Carolers, holding candles, sing "Nu Tändas Tusen Juleljus" while the flickering light mixes with their breath. A Scandinavian Christmas is coziness, warmth, and happiness like none I've ever experienced since. The memory is delightful. Really. Then she whispers, "That was the best time of your life." Under her influence, I am unclear which thoughts are hers, and which are mine.

Nostalgia can be cruel.

### Letting Go of the Dark Side of Nostalgia

The trouble with Nostalgia is she doesn't know when to leave *well enough* alone. With the innocuous memories out of the way, she segues to my recent past— my marriage. And this is where we pick up the revolving door scenario where she is at the helm. She shows me the beautiful, the holy, and the might-have-beens. I enter the city of Self-Pity, where I am queen. Nostalgia is a blessing and a curse, a double-edged sword if you will. I look back wistfully to a beautiful time, but the memories cut deeply. Susan Elliott in *Getting Past Your Breakup* describes the pain of looking back as "akin to putting [her] hand on a hot stove. [She] would recoil every single time." Yet we return again and again like a "dog returns to its own vomit, and the sow, after washing herself, returns to wallow in the mire" (II Peter 2:22).

For a grieving divorcee, Nostalgia shows up at the most inconvenient places: at church, at restaurants, boarding an airplane, or climbing into bed. She leaves gifts of melancholy and depression. Jane Austen had something wonderful to say on **Nostalgia is a blessing and a curse, a double-edged sword.** this subject: "Think only on the past as its remembrance gives you pleasure." Many times when I start thinking of the past with pleasure—those good things about my marriage, my home, the holidays, this happens:

Nostalgia's bony finger protrudes from her black cloak, and without a word, points me in the direction of the past and blocks my way forward. I cave. I go back to the darkness. But I get a glimpse of myself moving forward enough to recognize that this is where I want to be. It looks sunny, inviting, and promising. I'll get there—I just know it—but first, a few steps back.

The visual of the revolving door is exactly what I needed to turn myself around, to look at my life differently—to be different. I had to abandon the dark side of Nostalgia—this contrary woman of great strength opposing me at every turn. Dr. James Littles spoke these words in his Sunday morning class at The Sanctuary in St. Louis: "Sometimes, we must let go of nostalgia for all things to become new." He referenced II Corinthians 5:17. These words are life to me. I go back to them again and again.

> Sometimes, we must let go of nostalgia for all things to become new.

Research shows that our thought patterns cause deep grooves to form in our brains. A Google search for "mind grooves" yielded 807,000 results. The idea is this: our thoughts cause ruts in our brains; these ruts contribute to the thoughts we think. It's a vicious cycle. For me, it was always the same thought of wanting my old life back—I wanted the familiar because the unknown was frightening.

These thoughts never led to successful thinking or healing. In *Emotional Agility,* Susan David writes this maxim, "Who's in charge—the thinker or the thought?" This took my breath away. My thoughts often controlled me. I adhered to each thought. If they told me I would never heal from divorce, I believed them. In reality, I was deceiving myself. On the outside, I looked perfectly fine, but on the inside, I was a jumbled-up mess. Nobody knew how unhappy and unhealthy I had become.

I often woke up startled, as if someone punched me in the chest, with a dreadful thought. *I will never be happy again.* I ruminated on it and then determined that the thought was credible. Suddenly, everything was wrong in my world. I tried to minimize it much like I would a window on my computer screen and—voila! —it disappeared, but soon I'd see the article or unexplored site vying for my attention at the bottom right-hand side of the screen, and I'd go back to it. With one click, it filled the entire screen, and once again, I was lost in its contents. It was the same for my thoughts; I'd pick them right back up, rendering the deep groove in my brain, deeper still.

When I was in this cycle, sharing these thoughts with a friend helped me. Brené Brown called these friends her shame-resilient friends in *Daring Greatly*. Whenever I feel embarrassed or shamed in some way, I turn to these friends. On the lighter side, when I do something silly, these are the people who never make me feel worse. It seems I am always in need.

Years ago, my children and I volunteered at the Republican office during George W. Bush's second campaign. His chief of staff, Andy Card, stopped for a visit. The office manager bragged to Mr. Card about my sons' volunteer work. Thinking I deserved a little recognition as well, I took the moment to shine, but my words didn't come out as I had planned. I piped up, hand grasping his in greeting, and proudly announced, "and I'm your mom!" meaning rather that I was the boys' mother. Mr. Card was just as confused as I was; it was an awkward moment that ended in silent nods between us. I dismissed myself rather quickly and called my sister—a shame-resilient friend. She didn't gasp in horror. She didn't laugh, because she knew I wasn't ready to laugh just yet. She was simply that person hanging on the other end of the line helping me to find resilience.

Invariably, my shame-resilient friends tell me that these negative thoughts aren't credible. Having only one source in this instance—myself—I cannot be credible. I know this from all the college courses I've taken. The difference between credible sources and incredible sources earned me either a good grade or a poor one. Chiefly, one source is never enough for those source-loving professors. For help with my adverse thoughts, I turn to my shame-resilient friends and family.

> What joy is there in looking back to darkness, to nonexistence?

**Be Childlike**

Children do not toy with Nostalgia. They don't give ear to her. They don't brood over the past; they are too busy marveling over the present. We are reminded in Scripture to be more childlike; that is, if we want to enter into the kingdom of heaven. On that day, will Jesus say, "Oh no, no, no, you cannot enter, you are too adult-like. You aren't teachable. You no longer marvel over my creation"? *Please, no!*

It is from the following Scripture that I made rules of my own, reading into it a message that God did not intend. "When I was a child, I spoke like a child, I thought like a child, I reasoned like a child. When I became a man, I gave up childish ways" (I Corinthians

13:11). When I put away my childish ways, I lost wonder in the process. I made my own unwritten, hard-and-fast rule to life: take on Grief and never let her go; take on Nostalgia and nurse her like an infant, coddle her. Paul encouraged us to give up childlike behavior, not childlike wonder and humility. Matthew wrote, "unless you turn and become like children, you will never enter the kingdom of heaven" (Matthew 18:3). Wonder and humility must remain.

I desired to have the magic of childhood, to be curious again. I wanted eyes that light up with sheer delight over a butterfly that crossed my path, and to be awake to a little boy's fresh catch of the day. I wanted to hear, to really hear *The Four Seasons* by Vivaldi. But my eyes remained dark and unresponsive. I shrank from life. Four hundred years ago, Shakespeare wrote about looking back in *The Tempest*; he associated it with darkness, calling it a "dark backward and abysm of time," a chasm, if you will, a bottomless pit. What joy is there in looking back to darkness, to nonexistence?

### Leaving the Old and Embracing the New

My imagination served me well. How powerful and adept I was at hanging onto the old life. See, I thought I could mix the new with the old, thinking they could walk abreast. This was not wise, especially when Jesus, who knows something about everything, or rather, who knows everything about everything, required a "break with former things" (Matthew 9, Apostolic Study Bible). Jesus so aptly gave a lesson on garment repair and winemaking in the same chapter: "No man putteth a piece of new cloth unto an old garment, for it will not adhere to the old garment. Neither do men put new wine into old bottles: else the bottles break, and the wine runneth out" (Matthew 9:16-17, KJV). I'm not alone in this—the mixing of the old with the new. It has been a problem for centuries.

Lot's wife left us a gift as many of the ancients have. We are reminded in Scripture to "[r]emember Lot's wife!" (Luke 17:32, NIV). She failed to see God's provisions—the new life God had for her. Out of obedience she ran, but with each step came a refusal to accept the new life. In truth, I can't judge her because I am like her. In my loneliness, I looked back as well. Not only am I like her, but I resemble her husband as well in that I wanted to linger in my comfort zone (Genesis 19:16).

In a quote by Alexander Graham Bell, I hear the voice of Lot's wife warning me to take heed: "When one door closes, another opens; but we often look so longingly and so regretfully upon the closed door that we do not see the one which has opened for us." From her podium of sodium, she speaks right into my life. Let me be her voice to you. In your loneliness, you will be tempted to look back. But your healing isn't there. It's in the destination just ahead.

God's presence that leads and guides is found in the present—not in the past. I love this verse in Ecclesiastes 5:20 about how God doles out joy in the present. I find it particularly beautiful in the New Living

Translation: "God keeps such people [those people who accept their lot in life] so busy enjoying life that they take no time to brood over the past." The Apostolic Study Bible has this to say: "The man who finds contentment in what he already possesses receives an additional blessing from God." Perhaps that additional blessing is enjoying life to the fullest. We cannot enjoy life to the fullest if we are brooding over the past. I am my own biggest hindrance.

Paul wrote about forgetting what lies behind and "straining forward to what lies ahead" (Philippians 3:13). Hello! Paul was the guy who should have spent life in prison for the atrocities he committed. But there's always this: with that second chance afforded to him by God (and others), he created a new, beautiful life for himself. Most of us might spend the rest of our lives (or a big chunk of it) convalescing—recovering from the wrongs done to us by others, or the wrongs we commit. It's easy to get caught up in—what my friend Colleen calls—"doing penance" as a way to stay present with our pain. We lament and live with remorse for years. This is no way to live. We should look to the example of Paul, the chosen instrument of God who immediately started promoting Jesus after his conversion (Acts 9:15). He was able to "put off [his] old self which belong[ed] to [his] former manner of life" to make the necessary transformation (Ephesians 4:22). He was able to shake it off, that old life.

## Abandoning a Project

I had to abandon the original plans for my life to embrace the new plans. When God creates a new project, He doesn't keep reading from the old project manual expecting you to follow the old rules. No, He writes a new one tailored for you. I had been reading from the old manual—*The Manual of My Marriage*—for far too long. Since I was no longer married, this could not apply. The new manual began like this: "Remember not the former things, nor consider the things of old. Behold, I am doing a new thing; now it springs forth, do you not perceive it? I will make a way in the wilderness and rivers in the desert" (Isaiah 43:18-19). The way in the wilderness and rivers in the desert sounded promising. The Way Maker who "builds a road right through the ocean, who carves a path through pounding waves" cared enough to leave these comforting words for us—for me—to remind me that it's okay to abandon the old and make way for the new (Isaiah 43:16, MSG).

How will you allow God to create a new project? Since He sees the finished project, you must allow Him to trim and chop, sand if necessary, and even replace. In this way, you become new. Pure and simple.

From Victor Frankl's book, *Man's Search for Meaning,* I heard the clarion call to start anew from one

> You must allow Him to trim and chop, sand if necessary, and even replace.

survivor to another: "When we are no longer able to change a situation, we are challenged to change ourselves." Change was on the horizon.

I love this passage from the devotional *Streams in the Desert.*

> We linger in the lowlands because we are afraid to climb the mountains. The steepness and ruggedness dismay us, and so we stay in the misty valleys and do not learn the mystery of the hills. We do not know what we lose in our self-indulgence, or what glory awaits us if only we had courage for the mountain climb. What blessing we should find if only we would move to the uplands in God.

The mystery of the hills called to me.

On the upward climb, I asked myself, "Who am I?" The dreaded words spilled out of me: I am divorced. Single again. I had to accept the loss of the future I'd planned. I salvaged myself when I couldn't salvage the marriage.

I would make this new life a beautiful one. I was good at visualizing, so I imagined a bright future. A lesson on visualizing I find particularly charming is in the book *Who Moved My Cheese?* The author Spencer Johnson explains that by ruminating on the past, we cannot visualize a new life. Without visualizing a bright future, we are unlikely to move forward. There are many other delightful lessons in this brilliant book.

When the Master Builder decides to create a new project, we must abandon the old project. I remind you "all things work together for good" (Romans 8:28). All the good that life has to offer does not remain in your previous situation. There's good right here in the present too. I promise!

## My Transition

I needed to be intentional about making a change. More than anything, I wanted to create and embrace a new, beautiful life. I was tired of the setbacks I had encountered from reading the old project manual and living by its rules.

This was a visual that helped me think: out with the old (leave the past behind) and in with the new (embrace my new and beautiful life.) I transported myself to a recent memory, where I saw the Changing of the Guard ceremony at Buckingham Palace in London. The queen was nowhere to be seen, but that didn't deter the crowds. They gathered at her residence to await the ceremony. I, along with the crowd, reveled in its pomp—it was quite a ceremony, unlike any I had ever seen.

**I salvaged myself when I couldn't salvage the marriage.**

The precision of the marching was impressive, the band music, cheerful. Even the horses marched to the beat, looking regal, topped with guards of their own. All of this pomp was for the express purpose of relinquishing the duties of the old guard to that of the new guard. It was necessary (and an established practice) for the queen; it was necessary for a daughter of

> It was time to serve eviction notices to those crippling thoughts.

the King too. I needed to establish a practice of forming new thinking patterns.

If you need another visual, this one fits the bill as well: consider a mother bird with her foot securely in the nest and the other on her fledgling. With one swift kick, the fledgling either flies or falls to the ground. It was time to serve eviction notices to those crippling thoughts.

What this looked like on the outside: I sold my house and moved into an apartment. Memories came off the walls. I traded in the large family vehicle for something smaller. I stopped calling him—no contact was my rule. (Advice gleaned from *Getting Past Your Breakup*). I saw a counselor. I attended Divorce Care Classes. I devoured self-help books about healing, divorce, and losing a spouse through death. I started writing this book. I reached for my heart and cupped my hands to heaven as if I were handing my heart with all of its heaviness off to God in a relay. It was His turn to run with it. What it looked like on the inside: I created more space to heal. My broken heart started coming together piecemeal. What I discovered: I can be happy.

# Coaching Corner

Dear Friend,

It takes work to pull yourself out of the pit. Chin up—pull! Hoist yourself up to the next rung. Repeat. Keep climbing. The point is this: "Press on toward the goal for the prize of the upward call of God in Christ Jesus" (Philippians 3:14). Every day, take a step toward the goal.

Your destination is ahead, not in looking back. Brené Brown writes in *The Gifts of Imperfection*, "I now see that cultivating a wholehearted life is not like trying to reach a destination. It's like walking toward a star in the sky. We never really arrive, but we certainly know that we are heading in the right direction." Walking toward that star is like walking away from the pain of the past, away from the old life. As I walk toward that star, I pick up armor, just a few pebbles. Pebbles of encouragement like "find God every day" and "pursue peace" and "think on those things that are good." Positive messages like this reversed the deep grooves my thought patterns created.

It's time for a new motto. If you wish to use mine, here it is: *The present is much more pleasant.*

## Prayer

*Jesus, it is by Your help that I leave my past behind and press onward to a new life—a life of happiness and one without regret. Help me to find happiness each and every day. Help me to recognize nostalgia when it presents itself. Even though it is good to remember some things about the past, help me not to dwell there. I don't wish to live there anymore. I wish to live in the present for that's where You dwell. I put my hope, faith, and trust in You. I claim Lamentations 3:25 as a promise of Your goodness toward me. "You are good to those who wait for him, to the soul who seeks him." Jesus, I anticipate Your goodness.*

### Your Turn

ᴥ What steps could you take today to leave the past behind?

ᴥ What is it about the nostalgia from your marriage (or a former life) that causes regression?

ᴥ How can you redirect your thinking?

~ When faced with adversity, how can you best overcome?

~ When you look back on your life, how will you recount this time in your life?

~ How can you live a victorious life?

~ How can you find God every day?

~ What can you do to pursue peace?

~ Some questions have no answers. What question from your past could you release today? (Question adapted from Dr. James Littles' sermon "Don't Waste the Bread or the Storms.")

# 3

# Dependence on God

Aspire to a higher, nobler, a fuller life. Upward to heaven! Nearer to God!

Charles Spurgeon

In St. Paul's Cathedral in London hangs a painting of Christ. This sermon in a frame, known as *The Light of the World*, is a beauty to behold. On its ornate frame is engraved this verse: "Behold, I stand at the door, and knock: if any man hears my voice, and opens the door, I will come in to him, and will sup with him, and he with me" (Revelation 3:20, KJV).

This well-known altarpiece serves to remind its viewers that Jesus stands ready at the door of the heart of an individual, knocking. He will not force His way in. The door can only be opened from the inside. From the viewer's perspective, the door has not been opened for a very long time; ivy and weeds cover it. Yet, there He stands, hand on the door; a faint knocking can be heard, for all who listen.

In the painting, three different lights can be seen. A lantern illuminates His feet; truly, He is a lamp unto our feet (Psalm 119:105). A halo bathes His face in light and depicts His sacredness. But the light that speaks to me the most, however, can be seen in the sky. It is dawn; it is a new day. The Son looks out at the viewer with a hopeful look. Will the door be opened today?

When it came time to leave the cathedral, I didn't want to turn my back on this message. How moving is this call? I was that toddler several steps ahead of her parents who kept turning around to see if they were still there. I, too, wanted one more glimpse of this masterpiece. I love it for the artist's pure genius; I love it for the other visual it stirs inside of me—one not painted by William Holman-Hunt—but the one I concoct in my mind. See, I recognized that knock.

I opened the door. I moved the ivy aside. Disarrayed and drowning in sorrow, I invited Him into my pain. Divorce looked terrible on me. He asked, "What took you so long?"

> I invited Him into my pain.

## If Any Man Hears My Voice

*Psalm 93:3-4, New King James Version*

The floods have lifted up, O Lord.
The floods have lifted up their voice.
The floods lift up their waves.
The Lord on high is mightier
than the noise of many waters,
yea, than the mighty waves of the sea.

*Paula's Version*

The floods have overflowed the banks with vengeance.
One moment, I'm on the water's edge enjoying the scenery.
The next, I'm submerged and delving deeper
into its depths.
I hear my voice, muffled, pleading for life and breath.
The Voice is louder than the rising, rushing waters.
The Hand pulls me out of the deep,
Leading me to still waters. The shallow part, not far.
One deliberate step after another.
With the sand beneath my feet, I head
to the new day dawning.
Away from the pool of tears and its murky depths.
To a new way. A new life.

I was coughing and sputtering, spitting out water and sand, but alive, nonetheless. God made a house call at the crack of dawn and showed up with His bag of healing. He stood at the door, knocking; His voice gently inviting me to accept comfort, guidance, and peace of mind. It was a new day dawning for me too.

## And Open the Door

The presence of God, the Comforter, became my comfort. I looked to the unchanging Word of God when the circumstances in my life were changing and hopeless. He comforted me; His presence stayed with me at night when I felt most alone. I fell asleep to my hand on an open Bible, opened to Psalm 4:8. It brought comfort: "In peace I will both lie down and sleep; for you alone, O Lord, make me dwell in safety."

He had become my "Immanuel, which means, God with us" to my displaced heart (Matthew 1:23). Jesus understands loneliness: "He came to His own, and His own did not receive Him" (John 1:11). Picture a God who understands rejection and loneliness because He has experienced it. Try this: give God human qualities; picture Him sweeping you up into His arms. While you hold His embrace, meditate on what that would feel like.

My friend Jill sent me these words of encouragement. Newly divorced, she reminded the Lord of the Scripture: "Your word is a lamp unto my feet and a light unto my path" (Psalm 119:105). She felt at a loss and didn't know what next step she should take. All she could see going forward was darkness. God reminded her that she only needed enough light for her next step. She didn't need to see three months into the future. That was my journey through divorce too. It was best to not look forward beyond twenty-four hours.

Jill's words of encouragement reminded me of an encounter I had one evening shortly after my divorce. It included sparkling snow, lanterns, a pair of skis, a crackling bonfire, and time well spent with Tabetha, my sister-in-law. Living on the Minnesota prairie, winters are extremely brutal with temperatures often well below zero. On occasion, I braved the subzero temps to ski the trails of Buffalo River State Park. One of the most enchanting experiences I had was skiing the trails after dark. It was a beautiful trail that zigzagged in and out of the prairie and forest, bedecked in the soft glow of candlelight. Although the trail was dark, we could always see the lantern in the distance that guided our way.

From behind, a bright light illuminated the entire trail. Startled, we turned to see what it was. A man with an LED headlamp—a professional, no-nonsense sort of skier, unlike us—was coming toward us at breakneck speed. For a moment, it was bright as day; darkness could only be seen around the periphery of our view. When he passed, it didn't take long for the trail to grow dark, much darker than we had remembered it. We preferred the brighter light; it allowed us to see greater distances and deeper into the forest. But that is not the way of a candlelit trail. For a few moments, I stood paralyzed with fear for the darkness that enveloped me in the middle of the forest. I searched frantically for the glow of the lantern as my eyes adjusted to the darkness. That faint glow of the lantern could be seen in the distance—steady and constant—quite adequate for our skiing adventure to continue. *Dark, paralyzing, frantic times—that's how I would describe divorce.*

Barnes' Notes describes the "lamp unto my feet" in Psalm 119:105 to mean a "candle." He writes, "the Word of God is like a torch or a lamp to a man in a dark night. It shows him the way; it prevents his stumbling over obstacles, or falling down precipices, or wandering off into paths which would lead to danger or would turn him away altogether from the path of life." Through the gloom of my despair, I remained hopeful that the

33

brightness of day would return. If there was a "winter of despair," then there was a "spring of hope." Charles Dickens said it; I believe it. Hope was that glimmer of light that led to the very next lantern. And that hope for a better today brought my healing.

> Hope was that glimmer of light that led to the very next lantern.

As it turned out, we didn't stumble over obstacles; we didn't fall down precipices or take a turn down a wrong path. We always had sufficient light to get from Point A to Point B. A Swedish word "lagom"— its equal is not found in the English language—means "just the right amount." That was how I remembered God's presence in the winter of my despair. It was sweet; it was comforting; it was lagom.

This lovely evening ended in the lodge sipping hot cocoa and warming up by the fire. The memory is full of "hygge," a Norwegian word used to describe a beautiful night like this one, full of coziness, conversation, and candlelight—always candlelight. Making the necessary adjustments and using the Word as my mirror, my vision improved. Theodore Roethke shed light on this subject too when he writes, "In a dark time, the eye begins to see." When I opened the door, light filtered in. It makes perfect sense; Jesus is the light of the world, and "Whoever follows [Him] will not walk in darkness, but will have the light of life" (John 8:12).

My eye had begun to see.

## I Will Come in to Him, And Will Sup with Him

I found comfort in the visuals from Psalm 23. David was the guest of honor at a banquet and was served a "six-course dinner right in front of his enemies" (Psalm 23:5, MSG). What a visual! When my diet was primarily sadness and grief, God prepared a feast of well-being and abundance for me. Since we're on the subject of food, I came across Karen Le Billon's *French Kids Eat Everything* and was enchanted, being the Francophile I am. Overall, she had great advice to parents on teaching children to eat nourishing food. On her blog, she posts menus from French public schools where they follow a four-course structure (who wouldn't love this?): a vegetable starter, main dish, cheese course, and dessert. This meal in particular caught my eye and made my mouth water: cucumber with Balkan yogurt sauce; roast pork with gravy and lentil stew; Reblochon de Savoie (a traditional unpasteurized cheese from the Alps). Dessert was apple compote. This meal still lacks two courses described in the Message translation of the banquet in Psalms 23!

**God prepared a feast of well-being and abundance for me.**

God served up a generous portion of peace and comfort to David (to the reader as well) of Psalm 23. He seems to be saying, "Bon appétit!" It's a love story of God's provision that would stand the test of time. As the Gospel of John records, "I am the bread of life; whoever comes to me shall not hunger, and whoever believes in me shall never thirst" (John 6:35). I hear Jesus saying, "Come with a hearty appetite, Paula; you will be satisfied forever. Drink freely. Feast." What God had in mind for me was better by far than what I had in mind for myself. The latter included floundering, coming apart at the seams, stumbling backward rather than moving forward. God had me on the accelerated track to heal, and with that, He promised a future and a hope (Jeremiah 29:11).

## And He with Me

The Message translation of Psalm 23 reminds us that God is a refuge. "True to your word, you let me catch my breath and send me in the right direction. Even when the way goes through Death

> Death Valley was where Goodness and Mercy met up with me.

Valley, I'm not afraid when you walk by my side. Your trusty shepherd's crook makes me feel secure" (Psalm 23:3-4, MSG). Death Valley was where Goodness and Mercy met up with me. They had been pursuing me all along. But it wasn't until I experienced the dark valley that I noticed these two trailing alongside me. I'd like to think of them as my two friends. Goodness wanted all things good for me. Humble, never self-seeking, and kindhearted, she took in my suffering. Mercy extended compassion, blessings, generosity, grace and goodwill. These two friends embodied God and left me hungry for more of their time. The lesson from the twenty-third psalm is unequivocal—God adored me. He delighted in me, no holds barred. And delight—what a beautiful word!

I felt close to the heart of God when I read this Scripture: "He that dwelleth in the secret place of the Most High will abide under the shadow of the Almighty" (Psalm 91:1, KJV). When I was a young girl, for amusement, I would often try to stay within my father's shadow. When the sun was high in the sky, I would have to walk very close as his shadow was short. To stay in his shadow, I would walk backward with my feet planted firmly on his while he walked forward. I had to embrace him to stay put.

The sun would reposition itself, and so would I. One thing was certain; I had to stay close to my dad to be within his shadow. So close that I could reach out and grab his hand. Yet within his shadow, there were still parts of him hidden from me. I trusted that he wasn't leading me on a long walk off a short dock. Through the years, my father has always made me feel safe. He exemplifies what Henry Cloud and John Townsend define as a safe person in *Safe People: How to Find Relationships that Are Good for You and Avoid Those That Aren't.* The authors define a safe relationship by three things: it draws us closer to God (Matthew 22:37), it draws us closer to others (Matthew 22:39), and it helps us become the people God created us to be (Ephesians 2:10).

In God, I found safety. "I will say to the Lord, 'My refuge and my fortress, my God, in whom I trust'" (Psalm 91:2). I had to stay close to God to receive shelter and guidance. I found security—the very thing I was lacking—when I listened to the audio Bible as I fell asleep at night, when I read stories of faith and triumph, when I read about Joseph, the ancient, and when I considered Jesus on the cross. My five years of healing from divorce seemed minuscule in comparison to the betrayals Joseph faced.

In Sunday school, I learned Joseph was in prison, but he was always released during that same lesson, which led me to believe he wasn't in prison very long. Actually, he was in prison, not for days—like I had thought—but for years. He persevered in the face of huge obstacles. He kept a good attitude while his offenders were hard at work doing what offenders do best. He forgave them while they were yet causing his suffering. He said resilient things like, "You intended to harm me, but God intended it for good to accomplish what is now being done, the saving of many lives," (Genesis 50:20, NIV). Joseph's story reminds me of the ultimate example of resilience; Jesus on the cross forgave in real time when He said, "Father, forgive them for they know not what they do" while his assaulters were yet inflicting pain (Luke 23:34).

**Jesus on the cross forgave in real time.**

I love stories of resilience. To be okay with suffering, I had to find my "secret place." My secret place was within; it was where God removed my wounded spirit, cradled it to His own, like a mother would gently rock her baby—that was what it felt like at least. We need God's Spirit in our lives. That's how He communicates to us: His Spirit to our spirit.

God promised that He would make "known to me the path of life" (Psalm 16:11). For this promise, I was thankful. He would be my guide as I moved forward.

He only asks to be invited in.

## Coaching Corner

Dear Friend,

God wants us to depend on Him. Yet He also wants us to seek solutions to our problems and our roadblocks. An example of this in Scripture can be found in John 6:5-6. Jesus asked Phillip—even knowing what He would already do—"Where are we to buy bread, so that these people may eat?" (John 6:5). We, too, should question our own motives enough to cause us to search for an answer. And from that question, the disciples searched and found a little boy willing to share his lunch. From that lunch came abundance. And from this lesson, we know that God desires to be involved in the lives of humanity.

When the miracle was all said and done, all were confounded. "When the people saw the sign that he had done, they said, This is indeed the Prophet who is to come into the world!" (John 6:14). When Scripture uses an exclamation point, we'd do well to lean in. God Almighty was—and still is—at work among us.

My takeaway is this: God wants us to use our resources, but He also wants us to leave room for providence to move as well.

### *Prayer*

*Jesus, help me to listen for Your voice. In times of uncertainty, help me think upon Your miracles, and how You interacted with humanity. Help me to search until I find an answer like Philip and the disciples did. They offered You fish and bread. It wasn't much, but it was something You could use. Right now, all I see are my insecurities, my wounds, my imperfect self, but I offer it to You anyway. I pray that You will gather these meager offerings to Yourself and from it, create beauty. Change me to be more like You. I await a miracle, Jesus.*

### Your Turn

∾ How are you depending on God for your situation?

∾ How does God's Word light your path?

∾ Using the Bible as your mirror, how can you reflect God's glory in times of adversity?

~ In the winter of your despair, what are you learning?

~ What kind of feast is God preparing for you?

~ What is it about Jeremiah 29:11-13 that imparts hope?

~ According to this chapter, how is a "safe person" described?

~ When did you first recognize that Goodness and Mercy were walking along side of you?

~ What does resilience look like to you?

~ Jesus allowed the disciples to muse over how the multitude would be fed (John 6). What decision are you musing over today without seeking guidance from the Miracle Worker?

# 4

# Seeking Wisdom

So much is distilled in our tears, not the least of which is wisdom in living life. From my own tears I have learned that if you follow your tears, you will find your heart. If you find your heart, you will find what is dear to God. And if you find what is dear to God, you will find the answer to how you should live your life.

Ken Gire, *Windows to the Soul*

When my children and I visited London, our mouths were agape at the sights. Westminster was fabulous by day, but at night, this place was magical. The chimes from Big Ben filled the area with a beautiful, melodious sound. My son said in his profound way, "I hear you, Ben." We slowed our pace and listened. In the Big Ben clock room hangs this prayer:

All through this hour,
Lord, be my guide;
And by thy power,
No foot shall slide.

For the spiritual observer, the Westminster chimes suggest the call for God's guidance. The author of the

43

prayer, no doubt, intended Londoners to look to God for guidance. This was Solomon's idea too—looking to God for guidance, for happiness, to experience true kindness, to find the bigger life, and to pursue peace.

## God's Guidance

I leaned into wisdom and inclined my heart to understanding.

Solomon the Sage advised his readers to "[make] your ear attentive to wisdom and [incline] your heart to understanding; yes, if you call out for insight and raise your voice for understanding, if you seek it like silver and search for it as for hidden treasures, then you will understand the fear of the Lord and find the knowledge of God" (Proverbs 2:2-5). I needed wisdom; the knowledge of God sounded promising as well. In Lori Wagner's study called *Wisdom Is a Lady,* she describes wisdom as, "Looking at life from God's perspective: loving what He loves and hating what He hates." This kind of wisdom required me to take a step back and look at my divorce through God's eyes. Grieving was necessary for a time, but if He truly came to heal the brokenhearted, then I needed to allow Him to heal me (Luke 4:18, KJV). I leaned into wisdom and inclined my heart to understanding.

Over the years, I've taken special care to "know myself," as Socrates encouraged. He would be proud of my efforts. Three different personality tests helped in this

> **In truth I was apathetic, even judgmental, toward divorcees.**

endeavor. According to the Colors Personality Test, I am a Green. The test revealed that I am firm-minded; I seek justice; I'm a creative and calm person. The Enneagram test revealed that I am committed, responsible and suspicious. In Gretchen Rubin's framework for personality, I am a Questioner—things have to make sense. When I entered the world of divorce, nothing made sense. Minute by minute, I faced new thoughts, new feelings. I didn't know myself any longer; I was confused. The storm had seized my ship, capsizing it. This uncharted territory made me look to God; His lifeboat stood ready. I needed His help to find a new identity. Seeking to know myself began all over again.

Since I knew nothing firsthand about being divorced, I asked God for wisdom. Before going through divorce, I took little interest in it. In truth, I was apathetic, even judgmental, toward divorcees. I remember one incident in Walmart where a distressed cashier wanted to discuss her divorce. Her pain sat on her like a scavenger bird sat on its prey. Unable to break free from its massive talons, she shared her pain for temporary reprieve. I found

> **Then I experienced divorce, and my apathy turned to empathy.**

45

the scene disturbing—a vicious bird inflicting pain, a gaping, open wound with water seeping from her eyes, but it was her words that disturbed me the most. Since I didn't understand her immense pain, I became indifferent, avoiding it altogether. I was busy; I didn't want my ice cream to melt. My own ignorance led me to judge her: *maybe she wasn't a good wife*; *no doubt she was like that bad-tempered wife Solomon mentioned in Proverbs 25:24.* Then, I experienced divorce, and my apathy turned to empathy. I would now let the ice cream melt and cry with her. Having experienced divorce, I now understand.

"If any of you lacks wisdom, let him ask God, who gives generously to all" (James 1:5). We can ask God for wisdom—as we are told to—but I also learned that wisdom comes from seeking after it (Proverbs 4:5). When the Queen of Sheba heard of Solomon's wisdom, her curiosity got the best of her. She traveled a great distance to "prove him with hard questions" and to see his great wisdom for herself (I Kings 10:1, KJV). Her own understanding, no doubt, increased. Solomon confirmed this idea of mine in Proverb 13:20 when he writes, "Whoever walks with the wise becomes wise." It takes wisdom to recognize wisdom or as Diogenes says, "Wise kings generally have wise counselors; and he must be a wise man himself who is capable of distinguishing one." Sweet reason tells me that an encounter with wise people benefits those in search of wisdom.

The Queen of Sheba came to "trade for wisdom" (Matthew Henry Commentary, I Kings 10). She made a "grand and showy entrance into Jerusalem—camels loaded with spices, a huge amount of gold, and precious gems. She came to Solomon and talked about all the things that she cared about, emptying her heart to him. Solomon answered everything she put to him—nothing stumped him" (I King 10:1, MSG). Special care was taken so she would not be turned away. She certainly received her fill, so much so, that it took her breath away. Life changing ideas have that effect on me too.

### Wisdom and Happiness

I read a chapter in Proverbs daily. Solomon left us a gift, which I longed to have.

God's wisdom brought happiness. When her breath returned, she noted, "Happy are your men! Happy are your servants, who continually stand before you and hear your wisdom!" (I Kings 10:8). The Queen of Sheba came hungry but left full. As did others: "And the whole earth sought the presence of Solomon to hear his wisdom, which God had put into his mind" (I Kings 10:24).

Filled with gratitude for the things she heard, the Queen of Sheba said to Solomon, "Blessed be the Lord your God, who has delighted in you and set you on the throne of Israel!" (I Kings 10:9). This reminded me of the Scripture, "Blessed are they which do hunger and thirst after righteousness: for they shall be filled" (Matthew 5:6, KJV). I wanted to be filled with God's presence. I, too, would be like the ancients who came to Solomon for his wisdom. To honor God, Solomon's memory, and the Queen of Sheba's hunger for wisdom, I read a chapter in Proverbs daily. Solomon left us a gift, which I longed to have.

### True Kindness

The Queen of Sheba sensed kindness and deep understanding in Solomon. When I sense kindness and understanding in a person, I want to know everything about them. What makes them that way? Who are their mentors? Who are their friends? What books do they read? What are their hobbies? I want to spend time with them with the hope that, by osmosis, I will be like them. Much like Mary of Bethany in Scripture who sat at the feet of Jesus, I wanted to know more. Jesus embodied kindness, understanding, and love. Who wouldn't want to sit at His feet? Because of Mary's choices, the good part would not be taken from her (See Luke 10:42).

God's kind heart instructed the ancients to care for the widows and the orphans—those left without. Mary wasn't a widow that we know of, but she was a single lady living with her sister, and in need of kindness. God, being the lovely God that He is, left a little extra for Mary, much like Boaz did for Ruth in the Old Testament. Boaz invited her to eat with the reapers,

> He wants to leave you a little extra for those really hard days.

"and he passed to her roasted grain to eat. And she ate until she was satisfied, and she had some leftover" (Ruth 2:14). To today's divorcee—the 21st century widow—I'd like to say, God wishes to pass you some roasted grain, or whatever it is your soul needs to be sustained—He's on it! He wants to leave you a little extra for those really hard days.

"Who is like the Lord our God?" The reply shows His kind heart: "He raises the poor from the dust and lifts the needy from the ash heap, to make them sit with princes, with the princes of his people. He gives the barren woman a home, making her the joyous mother of children" (Psalm 113:5, 7-9). There is no one like our God: "His way is perfect," and "He is a shield for all those who take refuge in him" (Psalm 18:30). He reigns supreme; He is the "God of gods, and Lord of lords, the great, the mighty, and the awesome God, who is not partial and takes no bribe" (Deuteronomy 10:17).

For a literature class, I studied Homer's Odyssey, written in the 8th century BC. I now understand why it was incumbent upon the writers of Scripture to write that God was above all other gods. In literature, the mythical gods were known for their bad behavior and fickle ways. The God of gods, not fickle at all, loves me despite all my imperfection. He doesn't love me one day, and not the next. He never withholds His love from me.

God's heart is kind. And it is this sort of kindness that keeps me coming back.

## How to Find and Keep Wisdom

I rarely, if ever, use the word "cleave." According to Strong's Concordance, cleave in Hebrew means "to cling and to keep close" to God. "You shall walk after the Lord your God, and fear him, and keep his commandments, and obey his voice, and ye shall serve him, and cleave unto him" (Deuteronomy 13:4, KJV). This was repeated in Deuteronomy 30:20, except Moses added, "For he is thy life, and the length of thy days" (KJV). Why wouldn't we want to cleave to someone who is our life and the length of our days? This is a recurrent theme throughout the Bible as Joshua spoke these words when he was about to die: "But cleave unto the Lord your God, as ye have done unto this day" (Joshua 23:8, KJV). Matthew Henry said it beautifully in his commentary, "Let us hear the sum of the whole matter. If they and theirs would love God, and serve him, they should live and be happy." This has always been God's point: obey and you will have cause for happiness.

**Clear space for God to dwell.**

A prerequisite to finding wisdom is clearing space for God to dwell. Mary allowed space for Jesus in her busy day. In turn, she saw life from His perspective. Permit me to embellish the biblical account a bit: Mary ordered a Starbucks drink and was given permission to have a seat, to savor it, away from housework, away from others needing attention, away from the heavy burdens of life, away from noise, which enabled her to devote her attention to what mattered. I envision Jesus handing her His lenses, and saying, "Have a look." Maybe she saw green pastures and still waters. Whatever she saw, it was different from what Martha saw. Mary devoted her attention to Jesus; she understood that His "yoke [was] easy and [His] burden [was] light" (Matthew 11:30). Her work could wait. The idea of taking pause now and again is a delightful one. The key words here in finding wisdom are: Stop. Rest. Clear space. Devote. Thanks, Mary, for this lesson. (Luke 10:38-42).

## Choose the Bigger Life

In John 6, Jesus allowed the disciples to muse over how the five thousand would be fed. Calculations were made with their limited resources, and it was determined that they could not resolve the problem out of their own volition. The money they had would not buy bread enough for the crowd. They found a lad with five loaves and two small fish, but "what are they among so many?" (John 6:9, KJV). Ah, but it was something Jesus could work with.

I get a sense here that God has something bigger for His children. At least He did for the little boy with the five barley loaves and two fish who received a quick turn around on his investment; he gave all, and in return, he was able to eat as much as he wanted. "Give and it will be given unto you. Good measure, pressed down, shaken together, running over, will be put into your lap. For with the measure you use, it will be measured back to you" (Luke 6:38). The little boy likely brought leftovers home.

I've seen a poster circulating on Facebook where Jesus is standing in front of a little girl asking her to surrender her small teddy bear to Him. She's saying, but I love it. He's saying, just trust me. What she can't see is that He is holding a teddy bear much larger than the one she is holding. I, too, had to trust what I could not see, that He had my future in His hand. In the meantime, I would pursue peace. My health depended on it. I could not continue to live in anxiety mode.

## Pursue Peace

I am reminded in Scripture to pursue peace, to "[t]urn away from evil and do good; seek peace and pursue it" (Psalm 34:14). For an illustration, I'd like to call your

> **Seek peace and pursue it.**
> Psalm 34:14

attention to a dinner shared by the disciples and Jesus. But first, I'd like to share one such memory of my own. I'll take you to Spain, to a peaceful dining experience where I found happiness in the customs of this foreign country.

I have a special place reserved in my heart for Spain, for their customs, and one in particular—their late-night dining. As the hot Spanish sun sets, restaurant crowds gather. The clanking of dishes heard throughout the cobblestone streets is Spain's late-night call to dinner. When Americans are settling in for the night, Spanish families are sitting down for a feast. Spanish women fan their faces and those of their sweaty babies while they are fully engaged in dinnertime conversation. After dinner, families, dressed to the nines, leisurely stroll the cobblestoned streets, while kids play in the streets late into the night. I cannot forget those Spanish-style dinners we enjoyed together as a family. Luciano Pavorotti said it well: "One of the best things about life is the way we must regularly stop whatever it is we are doing and devote our attention to eating." Italians understood too; people living along the Mediterranean get it!

Rewind several thousand years. We are not in Spain, but in Jerusalem, not far from the Mediterranean. The disciples had just finished eating, also at night. It would be their last meal together. Jesus spoke words of comfort; He cautioned against a troubled heart. I love how He started this chapter with calming their fears; a great discourse indeed to follow a dinner. He understood human nature; He knows exactly what our hearts turn to.

**Jesus gave His full address: I am the way, the truth, and the life.**

In the way only He knows how, He offered His peace. He told them about His departure, but He promised a return. In John 14:4, He reminds them that they already know the way. But one was contrary. Thomas insisted on better directions; he needed an address to put into Google maps. He did not want his dearest friend to leave him. Then, Jesus gives His full address: "I am the way, the truth, and the life." He promised "another Helper (Comforter, Advocate, Intercessor—Counselor, Strengthener, Standby), to be with you forever" (John 14:16, AMP). He promised that He would remain with them forever, that He would not leave them as orphans.

My sister and brother-in-law adopted a little girl who was old enough to understand the sting of rejection. She asked my sister, "Will you be here with me forever? Will you always be my mother?" She understood better than most of us; she had been left an orphan "comfortless, bereaved, and helpless" (John 14:18, AMP). My sister made a promise to her that this would be her forever family. Jesus understood my niece better than anyone else ever could.

Jesus gave this assurance by offering his peace: "Peace I leave with you; my peace I give to you. Not as the world gives do I give to you. Let not your hearts be troubled, neither let them be afraid" (John 14:27). And to this end, we pursue peace. Just as God breathed inspiration into the authors of the Bible, He still breathes His comfort and peace into us today. I'll trade His peace for my anxieties any day; it's a good trade.

For it is in Him—not in my anxiety-ridden self— that I "live and move and have [my] being" (Acts 17:28). We are told to learn about Him and by doing so, we will find rest for our souls (Matthew 11:29). Without His peace, I remained locked into a life of anxiety, unable to forge ahead. I needed help to forge ahead.

## Coaching Corner

Dear 21st Century Widow/Widower:

Mary sat at Jesus' feet with her hands and heart open to receive all of God's goodness. Since God is a "rewarder of them that diligently seek him," she received (Hebrews 11:6, KJV). I am rewarded with wisdom, with an answer, with the assurance that all things do indeed work together for my good. (Paraphrased from Romans 8:28). If you seek for wisdom, you will find it. If you seek for God, He will be found of you too. "You will seek me and find me, when you seek me with all your heart" (Jeremiah 29:13).

Hide and Seek is a game I enjoyed as a child. Being the hunted was the most fun, but hunting had its rewards too. If I had a really good hiding spot, I'd begin to feel lonely and afraid that nobody would ever find me, so I'd start dropping hints, like hooting like an owl. Since time immemorial, God, too, has dropped little hints for us to find Him. Whether it is through creation, a pastor, the radio, or the written Word, God gets His message through to me.

In the same way, a sunflower is rewarded by its search for sunlight. As it is nourished by the light, so are we. My pastor, Michael Fennell, gave an on-point illustration about sunflowers that spoke of our need to find God in our everyday life. The onus is on us, not the other way around. This word picture has stayed with me for the human qualities attributed to this plant. As the sun moves across the sky, these tall, majestic flowers move their heads to follow its warmth, from east to west. The heads rotate back toward the east at night in anticipation of the sun's arrival.

The sun that lights our day points us to the Creator. As we follow the Son, we draw warmth and nutrients needed for spiritual growth. Jesus said, "I am the light of the world. Whoever follows me will not walk in darkness, but will have the light of life" (John 8:12). Ah! This though: "One sun enlightens the whole world; so does one Christ and there needs no more. What a dark dungeon the world would be without Jesus," and I love this last part, "by whom light came into the world" (Matthew Henry Commentary, John 8:12). Hanging on to the old life feels a lot like darkness to me.

For further study, read scriptures about pursuing peace. Start with my favorite verse in Psalm 34:14, "Turn away from evil and do good; seek peace and pursue it." Here I visualize turning away from my old life and its pain and receiving the gift God has for me: peace. He breathes His peace into my very being. How's that for a visual?

### Your Turn

- In the Greek, James 1:5 implies that everyone lacks wisdom when faced with adversity. How do you look to God for wisdom?

- How can you daily apply the wisdom of Proverbs to your life?

- How could you clear space for God to dwell with you today?

- In Scripture, we are admonished to pursue peace. What does this mean to you?

~ If God's yoke is easy and His burden is light, how can you apply this to adversity?


~ How could you be more like Mary and devote your attention to the Master?


~ Jesus cautioned against a troubled heart. What can you do to avoid being troubled?

# 5

# Humanity: Jesus in Skin

Christ has no body now but yours,
No hands, no feet on earth but yours,
Yours are the eyes with which he looks
compassion on this world.
Christ has no body now on earth but yours.

Teresa of Ávila

I have found connection critical in time of loss. Compassionate Friends, a support group for families who have lost children, speaks of the importance of reaching out through loss. Their motto is "We need not walk alone." Brené Brown in *Daring Greatly,* admits walking alone can feel miserable and depressing, but that we tend to "admire the strength it conveys and *going it alone* is revered in our culture." Revering such absurdities has no place in a crisis such as divorce. I invite you to nix this idea with me, and instead, connect. Sometimes we can't pick our own selves up off the ground. I sought the help of safe people: my family and friends; I attended divorce care classes and sought help from counselors. Brown says, "Sometimes our first and greatest dare is asking for support." Having been where you are, dear reader, I know

59

how easy it is to isolate yourself; I double dog dare you to reach out.

## Safe People

Henri Nouwen wrote *The Inner Voice of Love* during a particularly trying time. He describes a point in his life when everything came crashing down, which included his sense of feeling loved, his self-esteem, and his faith in God. Have you ever been there? He had little energy to live and work. In essence, he felt paralyzed by the anguish that took over his life. Consequently, he reached out to humanity. Nouwen said, "It is far from easy to keep living where God is. Therefore, God gives you people who help to hold you in place and call you back to it every time you wander off." The idea of being "held back" can be intrusive, like a bridled horse that's incapable of choosing its own direction; however, until we can see our situation with clarity, these friendly checks and balances are fitting and comforting. When we hit rock bottom, we can't see beyond ground level, but our friends, like giants, stand tall, scoping out the conditions. They see our situation from another angle. It's those different angles that lend new perspective. Since they have not been shaken by the storm, they hold us steady.

Good King Wenceslas, a Bohemian king, was such a giant. His story lends advice to those of us weathering a storm. In the process of delivering provisions to a poor peasant during a snowstorm, the king observed his page falling behind. The snowdrifts were deep, the winds prevailing, yet he instructed the boy to match his footsteps with his own: "Mark my footsteps, my good page, tread in them boldly, thou shall find the winter's rage, freeze thy blood less coldly." The elements can be cruel.

Through imagery—the raging winter and freezing temperatures—we are invited to feel the sting of this bitter night. It conjures up harrowing images of death by freezing. The boy was on the brink of a medical emergency, in dire need of warmth. In the footsteps of the king, the page found remnants of warmth; in the kindness of the king, he found the courage to go on. I was a lot like the page unable to move forward. See, when I was touched by *It*, like the childhood game of Freeze Tag, I froze. My family, friends, and faithful advisors were my teammates who, as the game goes, unfroze me with their grace, benevolence, and goodwill. Bit by bit, I thawed. Match your footsteps with the King, dear one. You'll find His subjects endearing as well.

**Match your footsteps with the King, dear one.**

### Good Family Vibes

My family were giants, too, that looked ahead when I couldn't. I think of them much like I remember my first reaction to traffic in the United Kingdom. I kept my head on swivel mode while crossing streets, as the inverted traffic was baffling. My family was in swivel mode; their guidance was essential to my healing. Their steady presence backed with private prayers reassured me. They tossed schedules aside, slowed their pace, and walked me through adversity. The ripping apart of "one flesh" of marriage was too much for me to bear alone. My sister was available all day, all night; I was that toddler who awoke needing comfort. She was Jesus in skin; my brother-in-law never lost patience. My brother and his wife loved me without reservation; they lit up when they saw me, saying little. At church their little one cried out, "Pawa! (Paula) I want Pawa." He'd cry until his love and desires were requited. I get it—I really do, little guy.

My dad pastored a church and already shouldered a heavy load. I watched as he placed me on the priority list. Over the years, my parents had no choice but to release many a bitter soul by dint of offenses, but they refused to let go of me. They cried with me, prayed with me. My dad brought flowers. For their time spent in the prayer closet, I'm thankful.

I derived comfort from my children. They helped me maintain a sense of normalcy in my rapidly changing landscape in which they alone provided beauty. My relationship with them was unchanging. Although my identity as a wife changed, my identity as a mother remained. It is from them that I felt love, which "always protects, always trusts, always hopes, always perseveres" (I Corinthians 13:7, NIV). One year into my divorce, my son married and gave me the daughter I've always wanted. I embraced sorrow with joy. In *Choose Joy: Because Happiness Isn't Enough,* Kay Warren writes, "Life is like a set of parallel train tracks, with joy and sorrow running inseparably throughout our days. At the exact moment you and I are experiencing pain, we are also aware of the sweetness of loving and the beauty still to be found." It is important that we embrace joy and sorrow simultaneously. Looking from afar, she says, "the two tracks aren't two at all, but one." Let us remember the wise words of Solomon: "For everything there is a season" (Ecclesiastes 3:1). The silver lining is this: depression and sadness stayed for a season, on one track, while hope and gladness ran alongside on the parallel track.

Even though my familial support remained strong, I still needed help from others.

### Friendships

> Their presence was a balm for the gaping wound in my soul.

Divorce can be very shaming, and I found that I needed to reach out to recover fully. Brené Brown says, "When something shaming happens and we keep it locked up, it festers and grows. It consumes us. We need to share our experience. Shame happens between people, and it heals between people." By speaking out to safe people, shame lost its death grip on me.

In times of adversity, it becomes clear whom we can rely on. I turned to wise people when I was undone. I reached out to several friends and acquaintances that had also survived divorce. Their presence was a balm for the gaping wound in my soul. I was living their story; and they, mine. Eric Grieten's *Resilience: Hard-Won Wisdom for a Better Life* was a nudge in the right direction. I understood so well his words: "those who went before us left us a gift." The guidance and support from those who had experienced similar heartache was truly a gift.

## The Body of Christ

Church was a place where I could just sit in the presence of God. I felt that God had no expectation of me; it was time to rest. I spent the first year gathering myself. I stepped away from ministry. People respected my pain. I am thankful for the gentle handshakes, kind words, and acknowledgments that they were thinking of me.

As I healed, I expanded my circle of friends. I escaped Minnesota's harsh winter and flew to sunny Barcelona where I studied Spanish. I made myself available to work with the missionary and the Pentecostals of Barcelona for two months. Outside of my comfort zone, I made friends with people I could barely understand due to the language barrier. The missionary family, the Harrods, helped me heal simply by being the Church. Returning home, I longed to do more mission work. Shortly thereafter, I accepted a position in Scotland for ten months, cooking for the students of Harvest Bible College. There I became the beloved American cook and was loved by so many. Their love and admiration brought healing. I made lifelong friends, and I fell in love with the United Kingdom in the process.

I reached out to like-minded people who loved God. I have met humanity—the Church primarily—at their best on my journey to wholeness. God has created such a beautiful refuge in the Church. The Church helps us and reminds us we are not alone. It doesn't even need to be the literal church that someone attends. My friend Cori reminded me that when I talk to her about my pain, my ideas, my prayers, I'm not just talking to a friend from afar, I'm talking to a part of the Church, a body member in Christ.

### Counseling/Divorce Care

I found a counselor who had a heart for God and family. A cancer survivor, he understood suffering. With his degree and many years of helping wounded souls, he earned the right to hear my story. As I bled out, he offered a listening ear and kind words. I focused on the heartbreak; he wouldn't allow me to hurt in silence. Instead, he invited me to feel, to speak up, to write. He embraced the words of Shakespeare, "Give sorrow words," and bid me to do the same. He took my words, softened the blow, and returned them to me with this charge: *humans have a wonderful and unique ability to heal, and as a physical wound heals, you will too.* Gentle reminders like these were gifts that stayed with me. He advised me to stay with the process. Those who don't stay with the process will shipwreck or walk around wounded. I walked into his office a "wounded spirit" and "difficult to bear" (Proverbs 18:14, KJV). God used him to cure me of that mentality. He allayed my fears. Godly counselors worldwide deserve high praise.

When I was in Scotland, I logged onto Skype with Carol Clemons, a Christian counselor. She became my counselor/life coach. Sometimes, you need help putting that one little thought to rest. She helped with those awry thoughts from afar.

Divorce care classes informed and guided me into the ways of healing. My goal was to take one thing away from each class, but that "one thing" became a treasure trove to ruminate upon and implement in the ensuing weeks. I can think of three things from divorce care classes that pushed me along:

1. Plan for one year of healing for every four years of marriage. For me, that meant I should allow five years to heal.
2. He was not my ally anymore. He was no longer looking out for my best interest.
3. *One is a whole number.* I found this statement surprisingly profound. In marriage, we focus on the two becoming one—this is beautiful. When you separate, either through divorce or by death, it feels as though you are incomplete—you become half of a person it seems. I, who had become one through marriage, became one singly, by divorce.

Divorce care also allowed me to meet others who found themselves in this gut-wrenching stage. We all experienced similar emotions, to varying degrees. Their stories validated mine. While they shared their hearts, they communicated compassion for mine. Things I couldn't express, they did with profundity. They shared with me three empowering, life changing books: *Rebuilding When Your Relationship Ends, Getting Past Your Breakup: How to Turn Devastating Loss into the Best Thing That Ever Happened to You,* and *How to Survive the Loss of a Love.* A lighthearted piece of advice from *How to Survive the Loss of a Love* is, "Snack on milk and cookies before bed." The point is to find ways to warm your heart in a crisis.

## Manna

CBS News correspondent, Scott Pelley, wrote an article about the Sudanese people who have been without food and water. Due to lack of roads, the UN World Food Program has been airdropping food to the people of Sudan. A poignant picture shows a Sudanese man looking to the heavens as crates attached with parachutes fall from an airplane. Pelley writes, "Hope arrived at 700 feet and 190 miles an hour." It's a story of humanity helping humanity. The biblical sojourners experienced a similar delivery of hope. God delivered manna, not by parachute or airplane, but it miraculously appeared like dew in the early morning hours. They were able to survive for another day.

> The people that were most like Jesus helped me the most.

Circulating social media is a poster of a bird sitting on a ledge with its head bent as if in prayer. As it is being pelted by snow, ice collects on its body. The caption reads, "Sometimes you just have to bow your head, say a prayer, and weather the storm." At times, it feels as though you have been left out in the cold, alone to face the elements. On such days, I charge you to read and commit Luke 12:6-7 to memory to remind yourself that God cares for you. If He cares deeply for a sparrow, then you, made in His image, are of inestimable worth. The people that were most like Jesus helped me the most; they did not allow me to suffer alone. In fact, when I picture God, I see these people. While the storm raged, humanity winnowed the ice and sleet right out of my cold soul.

Manna. These people were manna.

## Coaching Corner

Dear Friend,

Humanity reaching out to humanity is the theme of this chapter. Choose a motto that reminds you to reach out in times of loss. When you feel alone, link that feeling to your motto, and then adhere to it at all cost. Mine is, *Call a Companion*. My suggestion to you is find your tribe. Talk to the right people, a counselor, a pastor, a life coach, a "shame-resilient" friend as Brené Brown calls it. Above all, you need people on your team who will come alongside you, take you by the hand, and lead you forward. Stay connected. Find your tribe. We are all over the place! Left to itself, the hurting heart grows cold.

### Prayer

*Jesus, I pray that I will allow trusted friends and advisors to be Jesus in skin to me. Your way never requires me to go it alone. Your way includes faithful friends who will guide me forward to this new life You are calling me to. I pray that I will find remnants of warmth in Your people. Help me to find kind hearts that will help me heal. When I begin to isolate myself, send someone along my path that encourages me to reach out. These people help to hold me in place when confusion beckons me to wander from Truth. I ask for friends that will help me see adversity in a new light and from a different angle. I often need the stability of someone else's thoughts to carry me onward because my thoughts are often awry. Help me to find people who will be for me, like You are for me. Jesus, You are the hope for my chaotic world.*

### Your Turn

&#126; What sustains you in times of adversity?

&#126; Who is influential in your life?

&#126; Whom do you most admire? What qualities of theirs could you apply to your own life?

~ How has humanity been Jesus in skin to you?

~ Do you have safe people in your life? Are you a safe person yourself?

~ You get results from taking advice from someone wiser than you. How can you seek to have wise people on your team?

# 6

# Forgiveness

Everyone says forgiveness is a lovely idea, until they have something to forgive.

C.S. Lewis, *Mere Christianity*

I'll be straight up; I don't like doing things I'm told I have to do. It started when I was a toddler. My mother's words still echo: "Eat everything on your plate." I sat for hours staring at my plate, eating one pea at a time, gagging, then begging for pardon. My life got better, however, when I found the metal rails under our table with plenty of space to fit my peas, beets, and Brussels sprouts. As a grown woman, there are still things I find difficult.

Forgiveness is one of those things. Am I the only one? Or do I speak for humanity here? Forgiveness is a daily process; something I need to willingly offer whenever the need arises. Letting go is part of the divorce process, and forgiveness is intertwined with letting go. Just as I didn't let go of my twenty-year marriage overnight, I didn't forgive overnight either. As C.S. Lewis points out in his discussion on forgiveness in *Mere*

71

*Christianity,* you have to master simple addition before mastering calculus. So, I gave myself a break while I figured out how to forgive. I allowed myself to work through all of the emotions that came with divorce.

With the help of several Bible stories and Desmond Tutu's *The Book of Forgiving*, I set myself free and walked away from resentment—into forgiveness. I am no expert on this subject. I'm much more qualified to write the chapter entitled, "Holding a Grudge." Like you, I'm still learning. As preachers often say, "I'm preaching to myself here."

## Drop the Stones and Walk Away

It was the TED Talk of the day, without the lights, without the glamour, without the applause track at the beginning and the end. The great Orator sat teaching the crowd. A ruckus caused all attention to be taken from Jesus and placed on the woman who stood defenseless, unable to say a word, and even if she could, her words wouldn't matter much. The Law and her accusers demanded death by stoning. She had been taken in the act of adultery. Did she stand there partially clad or with no clothes whatsoever? I can only imagine the humiliation she experienced: the shame of standing in front of a holy God, the anger at the audacity of her accusers, the injustice of her sin broadcast in this manner to the crowd. Human injustice shakes me to my core. If I may take sides, I'll side with the adulteress here, preferring her sin to the sin of hypocrisy. With vengeance, her accusers demanded justice, and Jesus, oh so willingly, gave it. Rest assured, it wasn't what the men had in mind.

Jesus stooped down and wrote in the dirt. While the Creator went to work, the badgering, questioning and noise continued; they were much like toddlers who, after being told no, persisted still. It seems as if the dust of the earth gave Him the inspiration He needed to pronounce judgment: "Let him who is without sin among you be the first to throw a stone at her" (John 8:7). One by one, they walked away, perhaps dropping their weapons—the stones—at their feet.

**Be like God. Remember no more.**

Jesus bent over once again and wrote in the dirt. This adroit Sculptor sat once again at the drawing board. He wasn't done with His creation and perhaps needed additional inspiration like only creating gives. My mind went from the first man whom God formed in His own image from the dust of the ground, breathing life and soul into him, to the men Jesus breathed upon and said, "Receive the Holy Spirit (John 20:22). Ah, and this: "Let the soul which God has breathed into us breathe after him" (Matthew Henry Commentary, Genesis 2). God's desire for this woman whose sin was great was that she would breathe after Him, that His heartbeat would become hers.

The woman had likely resigned herself to death, but Jesus offered His life in exchange for hers. I'd like to think He handed over an "I owe you" promissory note to the accusers that read, "She's my child; she gets to live,

73

no holds barred. I'll pay for these sins on Calvary." Jesus pronounced no punishment, but required her to change, "from now on, sin no more" (John 8:11). Readily, her sins were forgiven. Long hours of penitence were not required, nor did she have to spend her days doing penance to prove her anguish and regret. God removed those sins far from her, "as far as the east is from the west," never to be remembered by Him again (Psalm 103:12). I don't see in Scripture that she even asked for forgiveness. That's the beauty of this. God knew her heart. Scripture says, He "search[es] all hearts and test[s] the mind, to give every man according to his ways" (Jeremiah 17:10). If God can "call those things which be not as though they were," then He can do the inverse of this as well (Romans 4:17, NKJV). Those things that happened, this woman's adulterous ways, God remembered no more. Be like God. Remember no more.

Paul recommends that we, too, forget: "forgetting what lies behind and straining forward to what lies ahead" (Philippians 3:13). Forgetting those things which are behind is a matter of volition. I cannot tell you how to forget as Paul suggests here, but we would all do good to stop remembering offenses. Stop remembering the hurts; this is how I moved forward. I trained my mind to stop remembering by "straining forward to what lies ahead."

I trained my mind to stop remembering.

# The Sting of Betrayal: Judas

Master painter Leonardo da Vinci painted the famous mural *The Last Supper* in the Santa Maria delle Grazie cathedral in Milan, Italy. I recently learned of da Vinci's struggle to paint the face of Judas Iscariot from Giorgio Vasari's *Lives of the Artists*. At one point, da Vinci was accused of passing the day lost in thought over his portrayal of Judas. The priest would rather he worked like the hired gardeners, "hoeing in the garden, never to have laid down his brush." Agitated with the constant goading by the priest for not understanding the nature of creating, he threatened to use the priest's face for that of Judas in the painting. As humorous as this may sound, he eventually painted the face of Judas in a way that "seemed the very image of treachery and inhumanity."

The disciples had to deal with their resentment toward Judas while they grieved the loss of their dearest friend, moreover dealing with the shock that a friend, one in their inner circle, had betrayed Jesus. When Peter addressed the one hundred and twenty, he retold the story of Judas (Acts 1). This wasn't new information; they knew the story well. Nobody could have possibly missed the cruel death Jesus was subjected to. That day, even the sky went dark at noon. The Apostolic Study Bible expounds on this: "The disciples still felt the sting of betrayal from one of their own company." Peter referenced the Psalms reminding the people about this prophecy, "My own familiar friend, in whom I trusted, which did eat of my bread, hath lifted up his head against me" (Psalm 41:9, KJV). Perhaps group-processing helped the followers overcome their resentment. The telling of stories, according to Desmond Tutu, brings healing. *The Book of Forgiving*, written by Tutu along with his daughter, Mpho Tutu, offers practical steps toward forgiveness. In it, they introduce the fourfold path to healing ourselves.

1. Telling our story
2. Naming our hurt
3. Granting forgiveness
4. Renewing or releasing the relationship

By doing these things, "our suffering begins to transform," Tutu says.

Peter tells the story—the one everyone already knew. Perhaps this brought collective healing to the group. It makes sense when we consider Tutu's fourfold steps to forgiveness. Since Peter didn't name the hurt, I will; it was a betrayal of the worst kind. The followers of Christ were left to make sense of Judas' mess. To help the group extend forgiveness, Peter appealed to logic when he shared the prophecy from the Old Testament. For the Scripture to be fulfilled, Jesus had to be betrayed by Judas and given over to Pilate.

The story of Judas didn't end well. With the betrayal money, he purchased a field (Acts 1:18). Scripture doesn't say, but I gather that the field did not bring happiness; for it was there that he ended his life.

Unable to renew the relationship, the disciples selected another to take Judas' place. Tutu's idea for healing and forgiveness is a powerful one. Apply it often.

The sting of betrayal can affect a person for years following the actual event. Desmond Tutu warns against hating the person who caused the pain.

> Many of us live our lives believing that hating the person who hurt us will somehow end the anguish, that destroying others will fix our broken, aching places. It does not. So many seek this path and it is only when they stand in the aftermath of destruction, amid the rubble of hatred, that they realize the pain is still there.

With betrayal of this kind, it would be difficult to trust humanity again. Yet the disciples didn't allow their hurt to close them off to others. They were all together on the Day of Pentecost. They chose a replacement for Judas. When we have been hurt, there is a temptation to build walls to protect our hearts, to give up on relationships, but ultimately, we need each other.

Consider this: Judas' betrayal made way for the most supreme act of selflessness this world has ever seen. It was foretold to happen. We didn't know that it would be one of us, one who studied under the Master, one trusted by the inner circle, one who sat near us in church, the very one who

**Judas' betrayal made way for the most supreme act of selflessness this world has ever seen.**

betrayed Jesus. The silver lining is this: it had to happen. The disciples, the family of Jesus, all those who loved Him dearly, had within them the ability to forgive, even when no apology was offered. The Bible does not say they forgave Judas, but because they moved forward, their actions say they did (Acts 1:14-26).

## What Forgiveness Looks Like to Me

The woman stood, straightening her body one vertebrae at a time, sore from the days of living small that had turned into months that slipped into years. She shuffled over to the heavy iron door and unfastened the lock with the massive key that hung from her neck, weighing her down. The door slowly swung open. She squinted at the light as she moved toward it. With each step, she thought, *I forgive I forgive I forgive.* The rhythm of these words, along with the sunshine she stepped into, warmed her soul and brought immense happiness. She felt as light and weightless as a buoy floating on the ocean waves. Lewis Smedes in *Forgive & Forget* said, "To forgive is to set a prisoner free and discover that the prisoner was you." The woman walked free because she set herself free.

## Coaching Corner

Dear Friend,

According to Matthew 18:22, we would need to forgive approximately twenty times in one hour, or four hundred and ninety times in a twenty-four-hour period. Although this is a bit exaggerated, the point is forgiveness should be our frame of mind. Forgiveness should roll off our tongue. When an offense comes our way, we should think *I forgive,* and then carry the offense no more.

I especially like this illustration of laying down offenses found in *How to Forgive When You Can't Forget.* It is a story of a monk, but that story reflects my heart for I carried a heavy load for too long. Two monks were traveling together and came to a muddy road where they met a beautiful young lady. She was disheartened by having to walk through the mud. She asked if they could help her to the other side. Both monks looked at one another astonished; they knew they were not allowed to touch a woman. The first monk scooped her up and carried her across. The second monk was quite disturbed by this. He watched as the monk threw protocol to the wind, abandoned his vow, and showed kindness to the young lady. Once across, the monk set her down.

The two monks continued their journey in silence. When they arrived at their destination, the second monk decided to have it out with the other. He reminded him that as monks they were not permitted to touch women, but he had gone so far as to carry her on his shoulders. The first monk retorted, "Are you still carrying that young girl? I put her down at the other side of the road, but you have carried her all this way." When you stop carrying your hurts, you lighten your load. Don't hold yourself prisoner. Set yourself free. Forgive.

### Prayer

*Jesus, I pray that I always offer forgiveness, four hundred and ninety times a day, if needed. Let me, with love, set my gaze forward. I wish to offer the gift of forgiveness wholeheartedly, without reservation. Let me remember that all humanity is flawed. Cause me to allow for people's differences and not allow any vindictiveness to fester within. Help me not to "hate [my] brother in [my] heart" (Leviticus 19:17). If I hate, I cannot live a wholehearted life. It affects my salvation, my health, and my well-being. Let me look to heroes of the faith like Joseph who forgave his brothers for the atrocities they committed against him. When Joseph could have punished his brothers, he chose forgiveness and love instead. Help me to see that inflicting pain on others never soothes my wounds. I pray that I exhibit Your grace, mercy, and forgiveness in adversity. May "all bitterness and wrath and anger and clamor and slander be put away from [me], along with all malice (Ephesians 4:31). Help me put bitterness far from me. Help me to humble myself through forgiveness just like you did, Jesus. I look to You as I move forward.*

## Your Turn

❧ How can you respond to evil with good? Consider Luke 6:27-28.

❧ How would you counsel someone in your shoes to forgive?

❧ Visualize letting go of the hurt and walking away from it altogether. How does that make you feel?

❧ What are some ways that you can forget what lies behind to press on to what lies ahead?

❧ With the idea that your obstacle is a gift, how does this make you look at your situation differently?

❧ Ann Lamott said, "Earth is a forgiveness school." It is a school we will never graduate from. What does this mean to you?

⋟ Forgiveness is choosing the future over the past. How can you apply this?


⋟ With forgiveness, we relinquish our desire to get even. How can you apply Romans 12:19 to your situation?

# 7

# Avant!

Forward ever, backward never.

Kwame Nkrumah

The man who is prepared has his battle half fought.

Miguel de Cervantes

When I lived in Glasgow, one of my favorite museums was the Kelvingrove Art Gallery and Museum. Its red sandstone building alone is a sight to behold, a city landmark that makes the Glaswegians proud. I went often to walk among the works the artists left behind. I loved the museum for its many galleries of art with paintings and sculptures from all over the world, relics from ancient Egypt, Scottish natural history, and a collection of European armor.

One suit of armor in particular caught my attention for its craftsmanship. Its resting place was behind glass. This well-protected armor, known as the Avant Armor, was constructed in 1455 in northern Italy. The word "Avant," meaning "Forward!" was engraved on the edge of the breastplate. The first time I encountered this relic of the past, I circled the vitrine several times in search of the engraved word. It was small and in an inconspicuous spot; I found it with the help of a docent. The message was clear, the direction set; this man in armor was to move forward. *Avant!*

> The message was clear, the direction set; this man in armor was to move forward. *Avant!*

How could this man in armor advance even a little when he was weighed down with heavy metal? Medieval armor for battle weighed anywhere from 45-55 pounds. This kind of weight is not the weight of a forty-pound backpack localized on the back. This weight is dispersed throughout the body, on every limb. I turned to the internet for understanding.

When Graham Askew was a young child, he visited the armories in England and pondered this same thing. In his adult life, his curiosity got the best of him. A biomechanics expert at the University of Leeds, he aspired to discover to what degree wearing a metal wardrobe would restrict a medieval knight. His theories were put to the test with historical re-enactors fully suited in armor. By walking on a treadmill and using a respirometer, the experts determined how much energy was being expended. It was found that men in armor expended twice as much energy with the armor than without it.

For perspective, try this: walk up three flights of stairs the medieval way. Place ten-pound weights on every limb and a ten-pound helmet on your head. Are you winded? I'm winded after walking up one flight of stairs carrying groceries. I've heard it said, "I'd rather break my arms than make two trips," and I wholeheartedly agree with this statement; apartment living helped me fully grasp this concept.

The point is that armor is heavy; we often want to discard it and shed the heaviness in its entirety. Similarly, that is how some view the pain of divorce. They place a tiny Band-Aid over the gaping wound, to temporarily soothe the pain. They find refuge in a new relationship, which ends up adding ballast to an already weighty matter. They end up worse for wear. Or they turn to drugs or alcohol, and substances that temporarily dull the pain, but the pain returns. Always. The person attempting to dull the pain is like the re-enactor I described walking on the treadmill, weighed down with heavy armor and getting nowhere fast. The goal is to move forward with the least amount of energy spent without spinning your wheels. We don't want to remain in neutral; we want to advance. I suggest that you put on the armor of God as Scripture suggests to protect your heart and mind and to stand firmly in the faith.

**We don't want to remain in neutral; we want to advance.**

But first this: If your divorce is relatively recent, you

may not be ready to move forward. I suggest you find peace meditating on God and His Word and read the previous chapters again. It is likely you still need to pursue refuge from others. Here's the thing: *armor won't help you heal*; that's what the Spirit is for. Armor is a pre-emptive tool. My friend Cori helped me to understand that "you don't put armor on people who are bleeding to death." If your heart is still flooded with pain, now is not a time to fight or advance. It's time to climb out of the pit. But when God, along with your trusted advisors, have helped you out—and you are ready—it's time to Avant!

My counselor said that in going forward, I *must* protect my heart. Here's the best method I found to do just that.

### Putting on the Armor

There seem to be two requirements that God expects from His children daily: we are to get our daily bread (Matthew 6:11) and to take up our cross and follow Him (Luke 9:23). In Ephesians six, Paul discusses other duties: the duties of children to parents, of parents to children,

**First and foremost, armor protects our faith and helps us stand strong in God.**

of servants to masters, and of masters to servants. Our duty to God is found in verse ten: "Finally, be strong in the Lord and the strength of his might." I find it interesting that Paul combined the duties of mankind in the same chapter that he spoke about the armor of God. I think he was implying that the "putting on of armor" was a duty as well—perhaps even a daily duty.

First and foremost, armor protects our faith and helps us stand strong in God. We are instructed to put on the full armor of God in Ephesians 6:10-18. We are to be strong in the strength of His might—in His ability to accomplish and to create. We are to draw strength from the same power that God used to speak the world into existence, in the same power that He walked with the three Hebrew children in the fire, that He raised Himself up from the dead, and that He is healing you emotionally.

The apostles were "clothed with" the power of God (Luke 24:49). Similarly, we are too. That promise is found in these words: "But you will receive power when the Holy Spirit has come upon you." (Acts 1:8). When we are filled with His Spirit according to Acts 2:38, we put on His power. Essentially, it is the power of God that helps us keep this armor in place so that we may stand. Just as God came to Earth to put on humanity, we have spiritual garments to put on as well. The Bible calls it "armor." Let's investigate this armor further.

First off, the belt of truth should be firmly fastened. Truth! It sets us free. The Apostolic Study Bible says it so well, "[t]he first specific piece of armor ("truth") is appropriate seeing that the enemy does not employ brute force but subtlety. He hides his fatal weapons under a fair cloak, thus making evil to appear good. His blasphemous lies have...the ring of enlightenment and profound wisdom." As I was healing from divorce, truth spoke volumes to me when nothing else made much sense. What is true? God is true. Jesus associated himself with truth (John 14:6). The statement "life is beautiful" indeed is true. If you've held your own child in your arms or stood at the rim of the Grand Canyon, you'll nod your head in agreement. And with truth comes all those other wonderful things that we are supposed to think about, "whatever is honorable, whatever is just, whatever is pure, whatever is lovely, whatever is commendable, if there is any excellence, if there is anything worthy of praise, think about these things" (Philippians 4:8). I like to break each one of these down, determine what they mean to me, and meditate on them individually. When you get a negative thought, H. Norman Wright says to counter negativity with truth and say, "Stop!— that's not true." Let truth be your guide. Fasten that belt.

**Let truth be your guide. Fasten that belt.**

Next up, don the breastplate of righteousness. It is a "righteousness that informs our ethics and enables us to become followers [imitators] of God" (Apostolic Study Bible). *Imitate God!*

The breastplate covers the heart, the seat of our emotions. Scripture makes a reference to our thoughts coming from the heart: "But what comes out of the mouth proceeds from the heart" (Matthew 15:18). Healthy emotions lead to resilience; wounded emotions have the power to destroy us. In a previous chapter, I quoted Proverbs 18:14: "A man's spirit will endure sickness, but a crushed spirit who can bear." A crushed spirit blights progress. And in regression is where our enemy would like us to remain permanently. We need to inform our hearts that "A cheerful heart is good medicine, but a crushed spirit dries up the bones" (Proverbs 17:22, NIV). If our hearts remain unprotected, they become bitter. Who will protect our hearts if we don't? If we are to imitate God, then we can't stay in the pit of darkness. Jesus was allowed three days in the grave, then rose again to new life. We, too, must move forward. Maybe a sturdy pair of figurative shoes will provide support.

The soldier is instructed to have "shoes for [his] feet, having put on the readiness given by the gospel of peace" (Ephesians 6:15). Readiness or being prepared, as the King James Version puts it, suggests a mind that is mentally prepared, even though Paul references shoes here. Odd, I know. He wanted our minds to be prepared for the very *next* thing, as well as having a sturdy pair of figurative shoes so that we would be able to stand. By putting on this armor, Paul is helping us to see that there is a battle raging. But even in a battle, there are times of peace. The Gospel gives us peace. If we warred all the time, that would be exhausting. "Ponder the path of your feet; then all your ways will be sure" (Proverbs 4:26). Scriptures

> But even in a battle, there are times of peace. The Gospel gives us peace.

with "if" and "then" messages make me lean in. *If* you ponder the path of your feet, *then* your ways will be sure.

The shield of faith alludes to the power of prayer to quench a fiery warfare that is waged against us. Paul writes, "take up the shield of faith, with which you can extinguish all the flaming darts of the evil one" (Ephesians 6:16). I love this word picture: the evil one fires a shot; the shield that "cover[s] a great part of the body" extinguishes these fiery darts as they arrive (Pulpit Commentary). If we don't employ the shield, those flaming darts affect our mind and we become "inflam[ed] with lust, pride, revenge, and other evil feelings" (Pulpit Commentary). Praying the shield of faith is to say to Satan, "Denied! Try a different tactic; that one didn't work."

Next, the helmet of salvation protects our mind from the thoughts that hinder forward movement. The mind is the seat of our thoughts, anxieties, and ideas. Prayers of protection over our mind help to rid us of fears. "For God gave us a spirit not of fear but of power and love and self-control" (II Timothy 1:7). I really like what H. Norman Wright has to say about this Scripture: "Memorizing and dwelling upon this Scripture can help bring order to your thought life, and as a result, improve your relationships, health, and happiness." He also says that our thoughts are often "more adversary than ally. Left unchecked, our thought life can become our own worst enemy, poisoning us from within." You can easily see why our minds should be protected by prayer. To apply the helmet of salvation is to apply all the Scriptures that give us thoughts of peace.

Lastly, pick up the "sword of the Spirit, which is the word of God" (Ephesians 6:17). MacLaren's Expositions reads, "It is worth noting that there is only one offensive weapon mentioned—the sword of the spirit. All the rest are defensive—helmet, breastplate, shield, girdle, and shoes." The Word of God instructs us to pray at all times in the Spirit. To that end, this foot soldier, now fully clothed must stay alert "with all perseverance, making supplication for all the saints" (Ephesians 6:18). To stay alert, "Let your eyes look directly forward, and your gaze be straight before you" (Proverbs 4:25). *Before you.* Forward movement. Did you catch that?

> Let your eyes look directly forward, and your gaze be straight before you.
> Proverbs 4:25

### "That you may be able to stand against the schemes of the devil."

What would those schemes look like? The devil fights against those very things that God requires, such things like searching the Scripture for our daily bread and picking up our cross—dying to self—to follow Him. Without doing these things daily, we will lack the motivation it takes to move forward. In MacLaren's Exposition, he says the "main part of our warfare consists in defense, in resistance, and in keeping what we have, in

## It takes commitment to change our thoughts and behavior.

spite of everybody, men and devils who attempt to take it from us." Scripture admonishes us to "hold on to what you have, so that no one may seize your crown" (Revelation 3:11). You may encounter a few individuals who neither want you to be happy nor to move forward. Recognizing them for who they are is half the battle. My reply to those people, "I saw what you did there, and it's not working. Step aside. I'm moving right along."

Can we pause here a moment to imagine this man in armor? The imagery Paul uses in Ephesians six evokes quite a picture. This idea of using armor to protect our minds came to him while in prison. Perhaps it was the prison guards or the men who delivered his meals who started him thinking about armor. All the same, Paul describes the Roman armor of that day, and that, in turn, reminds him of the enemy of our soul. We should commit to pray each piece of armor into place to protect our minds from the onslaught of the enemy and to help us move forward. It takes commitment to change our thoughts and behavior.

When Hernán Cortés, a Spanish conquistador, reached the shores of Mexico, he ordered his ships to be burned. Burning their only means of return required total commitment by his men. I wonder what went through their minds. Were they onboard with this idea? Perhaps there was already talk of retreat. Who wouldn't want to return to the comforts of home? Without options, they stayed the course. Subsequently, the only choice they had was to put one foot in front of the other, walk toward the new land away from the burning ships, away from their smoldering safety net. They moved forward and eventually conquered the Aztec empire.

## When We Get Off Track

Because we aren't so adept at burning our ships and using the armor of God, we easily get off track. We drop that heavy armor. It slows us down. To our modern thinking, slow is bad. A slow-paced driver will push most of us over the brink of insanity. But slow is not always bad. With a slower response comes more time to think—to really think—about factors that hinder forward movement and those darts that get us off track. It is better to be slow and protected, rather than fast and unguarded, as my friend Cori advised me.

**It is better to be slow and protected, rather than fast and unguarded.**

The direction in which I set my feet is the way I end up heading every time. Although not profound, it made me think about Lot who pitched his tent toward Sodom. Shortly thereafter, he became an inhabitant; he sat at the gate, which implies that he had significance in the city. He traded his tent for a sturdier house, something more permanent (Genesis 19:4). As it turns out, this proved to be a bad decision for him and his family. Ultimately, he lost his wife because of the direction he chose for his family. Lot got off track.

"Forward ever, backward never" is a quote that I put on repeat whenever I feel as if I am going backward or getting off track. Henri Nouwen wrote a beautiful piece about getting off track. He tells his readers that they shouldn't get discouraged when they get off track, thinking they've lost everything. He says, "What you have gained, you have gained." You haven't lost everything. That right there is a gem to hold on to when you feel you've gone back a few steps. Take a moment to notice how far you've come.

*Ways We Move Backward: Unhealthy Love.* Wanting what we can't have is a sure recipe for disaster. Terence, the Roman poet, said, "The less my hope, the hotter my love." What I know personally about love is that it can be beautiful, but love at its worst is uncouth and ugly. It can be the opposite of all the descriptions of love found in I Corinthians 13, the love chapter. Here is looking at love in its inverse: it is impatient and unkind; it insists on its own way; it brings resentment; it causes intense moments of jealousy; it is prideful and arrogant. This kind of love, which isn't love at all, serves to level you and bring you down.

Solomon, the good writer and communicator that he was, understood the concept of looking at a matter from two different angles. He paired love with hatred: "Hatred stirs up strife, but love covers all offenses" (Proverbs 10:12). Hatred and love, oh, what a thin line between the two! Science editor, Steve Connor, writes that the "hate circuit shares something in common with the love circuit" in brain scans. In his article, Connor quotes Professor Semir Zeki regarding the similar natures of love and hate: "the findings could explain why both hate and romantic love could result in similar acts of extreme behavior—both heroic and evil." Extreme behavior—unhealthy love—has the tendency to show up during a divorce. Removing love from the equation is no easy process. Experiencing unrequited love is a recipe for disaster. Beware.

*Ways We Move Backward: Comparison.* Theodore Roosevelt said, "Comparison is the thief of joy." With comparison come the feelings of inadequacy and the mentality that I will never be enough. Comparing myself to other divorcees was a sure way to spiral downward into the deep abyss of depression. Anne Lamott in her TED Talk "12 Truths I've Learned from Life and Writing" says, "Try not to compare your insides to someone else's outsides. It will only make you worse than you already are." Although humorous in her delivery, the message speaks volumes. I compared my miserable self to someone else's healed self.

We are miserable when we think we should be someone we aren't. I've heard it said this way too: *don't compare someone's best day to your worst day.* Ah, let that sink in. But this may very well be my favorite: *Don't compare a friend's Facebook vacation photos to your "I'm-just-getting-out-of-bed" look.* In *The Artist's Way,* Julia Cameron says that film students usually "don't

**The first step to coveting starts with comparison.** compare [their] student films to George Lucas's student films. Instead, [they] compare them to *Star Wars.*" This type of comparison can steal the joy right out from underneath us. Have you seen the tablecloth trick where the tablecloth is removed with one quick jerk while the dishes stay put, albeit somewhat shaken? That's what I think of this kind of comparison. The joy is removed right out from underneath us, leaving us a little shaken.

Let's not forget the final commandment of the Ten Commandments given to humanity by God Himself, "You shall not covet" (Exodus 20:17). This commandment warns against wanting something that isn't yours. The first step to coveting starts with comparison—I'm sure of it. I have compared my unmarried self to the memory of my married self, especially at times when I enter a restaurant, church, or a museum alone. Two is better than one, isn't that what the Bible says? And that's when I begin to covet. Can you banish your desire for this person altogether since he/she doesn't belong to you anymore? Can you stop coveting your old life? This will help you to move along.

*Ways We Move Backward: Feeling Hopeless.* Remaining hopeful in times of difficulty is crucial. Without hope, we regress. I compared the chaos of divorce to that of the destruction of a hurricane that devastates an entire city. Nothing leaves a person more hopeless than being displaced and losing your home with all its familiarities. The silver lining came with all the people who thrust hope upon me. I learned that although I couldn't change my circumstances—remove myself from the path of the hurricane—I could change how I looked at those circumstances.

An interesting phenomenon occurred with Hurricane Irma. The waters from the shoreline were pulled toward the center of the storm, leaving the ocean floor exposed. The storm was so powerful that it changed the shape of the shoreline temporarily. (How I would have loved to comb the beach that day!) Warnings went out to area residents to exercise caution as the waters often return with fury. This is what divorce does: it changes the landscape of your life, and it exposes your pain for all to see, albeit temporarily. Desmond Tutu said, "Hope is being able to see that there is light despite all the darkness." How do you know it's dark if you don't know what light is?

**Hope replaced despair.**

I appreciate how Kaitlin Roig-DeBellis, the teacher who survived the Sandy Hook Elementary School shooting, found hope in her darkness. She desired to move forward from that terrible event. She asked two questions of herself: "how could she ensure the deeds of a madman did not prevent her from moving forward to live a good life? And how would she regain the sense of control he took from her?" She said that these questions

97

"led [her] in everything [she] did." In the course of time, her sanity returned. Hope replaced despair. My personal story was very different from hers. I'm cautious to compare my story to hers, but Roig-DeBellis so graciously said, "Pain is pain and sadness is sadness and loss is loss and we are all connected in this."

These questions Roig-DeBellis asked of herself guided her. Asking questions of oneself is a powerful way to determine how well we are doing, how well we are moving forward. *How am I progressing today?* I ask myself on occasion.

Hope has an uncanny ability to pass between people and to grow rapidly inside of you.

Benjamin Franklin implemented a project to help improve his life. He made a chart with thirteen virtues. Each evening he checked off how well he did with each of these. For example, on humility, he aimed to imitate Christ or Socrates. Each evening, he'd place an asterisk next to this virtue, either he managed to imitate Christ or Socrates, or he didn't. In this manner, he kept track of his progression through the virtues. Some days this scientist, inventor, author, musician, and politician would fail, so he left the column blank. This is what I imagine. He would turn out the light and go to sleep, with the hope that tomorrow would be a better day.

The idea here is self-improvement. In it lies hope—hope for a better day, hope for a better tomorrow. "Hope deferred makes the heart sick, but a desire fulfilled is the tree of life" (Proverbs 13:12). This new life I'm embarking on will fulfill a desire of mine—to be whole again. From this Scripture, I get a visual of a large tree teeming with life and all things that pertain to happiness—hope, its foundation. If you aren't at the hopeful stage yet, then embrace these words by Marilynne Robinson in her beautiful novel *Gilead,* "Hope deferred is still hope." Grab onto a tiny glimmer of it when it passes by. Hope has an uncanny ability to pass between people and to grow rapidly inside of you.

*Ways We Move Backward: Unhealthy Thinking.* When I was a teenager, my grandmother, my siblings and I took a road trip from North Dakota to Texas to meet my parents. We were in the middle of nowhere when we felt a thump, heard a loud noise, and saw smoke in the rearview mirror. We had experienced a blowout. There we sat in a hot car until help arrived. We rode with a trucker to a nearby gas station, while he told us horror stories of how people disappeared in situations like ours. He was a modern-day "Job's comforter," making little effort to console us. By the time the tire was changed, we were shaken and hours behind schedule. Years later, my thoughts had become like this flat tire. I could neither move forward, nor could I slide in reverse. I had come to a grinding halt. My whole self was in arrears. I understood my potential, but I remained in inertia. What I knew about Newton's Third Law of Motion—the law of inertia—was that I couldn't remain at rest with the forces behind propelling me forward. I was being acted upon by my friends and God to move forward. The laws of science win every time.

Nobody can advance by looking in the rearview mirror. You'll wreck your life and all those traveling with you.

When my friend Jill was going through divorce, her faithful friend advised her to stop living her life looking in the rearview mirror—that is to stop ruminating on the past. Sure, there may be some stunning views looking back, but those views just keep getting smaller. Nobody can advance by looking in the rearview mirror. You'll wreck your life and all those traveling with you.

Advancing requires focus on the prize. How I love to get a prize for my hard work. "Those who are victorious will inherit all this, and I will be their God and they will be my children" (Revelation 21:7, NIV). Although this Scripture is referring to heaven, I thought of the new life I was seeking, the happier one unencumbered by negative thoughts. That was the prize I looked to. By holding on to your negative thoughts, it will put you behind the wheel of a car with a flat tire. You won't get very far. The carrot dangling in front of you—the prize— is your new life. Excuse me, Ma'am, excuse me, Sir, the phone is ringing, and it's for you. Your new life is calling. Will you answer?

We face obstacles any time we try to move away from a bad habit into a good one—moving forward with a new idea, mending a hurt, or putting greater effort into being more Christ-like. To overcome this, I had to change my thinking, just as my grandmother's flat tire had to be changed and thrown out. To do just that, I considered Susan David's words in *Emotional Agility* on established thought patterns. She says,

> People frequently die in fires or crash landings because they try to escape through the same door they used when they entered. In their panic, they rely on an established pattern instead of thinking of another way out. In the same manner, our suffering, our disengagement, our relationship challenges, and our life difficulties are almost never solved by thinking in the same old, automatic way.

The apostle Paul suggests this antidote to change negative thought patterns: "Fix your thoughts on what is true, and honorable, and right, and pure, and lovely, and admirable" (Philippians 4:8, NLT). In *A Better Way to Think,* H. Norman Wright says, "If you simply try to empty your mind of negative thoughts, but fail to replace them with positive thoughts, the negative thoughts will return." He compares the danger of emptying our minds of negative thoughts to emptying our homes of all that we

> There are miles of happiness that lie ahead. Hustle to that new life.

possess. Eventually we begin to feel uncomfortable without furniture, without our things, without our clothes. So, we return for the comforts of home, just like we return to those negative thoughts because, he says, "You're comfortable with all those thoughts, bad as they are." But negative thinking leads to stasis and stagnation. Instead, I will trust what is not seen (Hebrews 11:1). I will trust in the unknown of my new life that lies ahead. There are miles of happiness that lie ahead. Hustle to that new life.

There's a whisper on the night-wind,
there's a star agleam to guide us,
And the Wild is calling, calling...
let us go.

Robert William Service

## Coaching Corner

Dear Friend,

In *Daring Greatly,* author Brené Brown popularized the speech "The Man in the Arena" by Theodore Roosevelt.

> It is not the critic who counts; not the man who points out how the strong man stumbles, or where the doer of deeds could have done them better. The credit belongs to the man who is actually in the arena, whose face is marred by dust and sweat and blood; who strives valiantly; who errs, who comes short again and again.

This, to me, is what moving forward to that new life is about. It's about putting on the armor and fighting your way clear through to the other side. You may have to suit up and stay in the arena a bit longer, my friend.

Having spent three summers in Spain, I visualize a Spanish matador standing in a bullring poised to fight. The matador's "face is marred by dust and sweat and blood." His enemy has already left its mark and now must be conquered. The drill is to kill the bull. The only options the matador has are fight or flight. And fight is what he has been trained to do. The mind, too, must be prepared for battle.

Much like I greeted my grief in Chapter 1 with "Hello old life," I gave my negative thoughts a label as well. I called those negative thoughts "A Bull in a China Shop." This destructive bull of mine shows up at the most inconvenient of times and wreaks his havoc in my mind. Just when I get the imaginary dishes displayed, the bull is back again, knocking teacups off the wall. Call your enemy what you will, but definitely give him a title. Then as he returns, I greet him with "Ah, Mr. Bull in a China Shop, back so soon? I was expecting you. I'm ready for you this time."

The apostle Paul offers this antidote to be spiritually victorious: dress yourself in the armor of God. Pray each piece of armor into place as it relates to you. My hope and prayer is that you will turn yourself around post haste. Only you can turn yourself around. Persevere, my friends! Stay in the arena. Fasten that armor. Fight forward. Forward ever, backward never.

## Prayer

*Lord, I desire more than anything to be strong in You. I want to be able to stand firm against the schemes of the devil. I understand that the devil starts wreaking his havoc in my mind first. Once my mind is teeming with his negativity, I lack motivation to move forward. As I fasten the belt of truth, I pray that truth will be my guide. Without truth, I wander aimlessly. I cover my heart with the breastplate of righteousness in an attempt to "keep my heart with all vigilance for from it flows the springs of life" (Proverbs 4:23). I place the gospel of peace on my feet and await marching orders. Help me to use the shield of faith to protect me from the flaming darts of loneliness, insecurity, and fear. Thank you for the helmet of salvation. Cause me not to dwell on the past but instead to keep my thoughts on You. I rest in the knowledge that I'm secure in Your hand. Help me to take up the sword of the Spirit to be surrounded by Your words daily. When I don't know how to pray, help me to pray in the Spirit (Romans 8:26). Jesus, You are the way, the truth and the life (John 14:6). The schemes of the devil darken my way causing me not to see Your light. Your way brings happiness, peace, and healing. Thank you, Jesus.*

## Your Turn

❧ What does moving forward look like to you? Visualize it.


❧ When you visualize moving forward, what makes you feel happy? What makes you feel anxious?


❧ Now that you are certain you cannot return to your old life, what strategy do you have to move forward?


❧ What is stopping you from moving forward?


❧ Consider Philippians 4:8. How could you incorporate this verse into your everyday life

# 8

# My New Life

Barn's burnt down—
now
I can see the moon.

When new beautiful thoughts began to push out the old hideous ones, life began to come back to him, his blood ran healthily through his veins and strength poured into him like a flood.

Frances Hodgson Burnett, *The Secret Garden*

When I look in the mirror, I see kintsukuroi.

Kintsukuroi is a Japanese process of repairing a piece of pottery by using gold or silver lacquer. Perhaps you've seen posters circulating the social channels, showing an ordinary piece of pottery made extraordinary. Its cracks have been repaired with gold. This glue of sorts holds the seams together, creating a new piece that glimmers at the seams. No one piece looks the same, as no one piece breaks identically. What were damaged goods has been pieced back together and is now a beautiful piece of art.

## Broken objects are stunningly beautiful.

The art of kintsukuroi is different from stained glass, but in some ways similar. Both artists work with broken materials. My friend Cori reminded me that stained glass is intentionally cut so that each piece forms parts of the whole. The whole sheet of glass must first be broken. One broken piece of glass after another fits into the entire piece. This reminded me of a visit to the Basilica of the Sagrada Familia in Barcelona, Spain. The stained glass displays there are astonishing. They illuminate entire areas of the cathedral, from floor-to-ceiling. I was told to go early in the day to see the magical display by the sun. The brilliant light from without bathed me from within with every color imaginable. I walked through the colors that streamed in, mouth agape.

Broken objects are stunningly beautiful.

There are times in life when we are so broken that we cannot put the pieces back together. This is where we let the gold fill where the cracks are. And God's healing touch enters the picture. Those loving hands—very familiar with creating—get to work. God's glory, not gold, fills the cracks. We don't insist that the pieces fit together perfectly. My artist friend Colleen said, "the cracks reflect someone's love and time and hands [human touch], putting something back together that they believed had worth. When the brokenness has worth, not only does the mender take the time and effort to fix it, he fixes it with pure gold, making the broken shards stunningly beautiful." The idea here is that broken things have purpose, and that purpose may change from what it once was. The piece of pottery may not be able to hold food or liquids any longer. Even if we don't know the "why," we can allow our brokenness to become something beautiful.

Out of our brokenness, God creates.

Humanity in all its brokenness and frailty moves the heart of God. Just as we are moved by the stories of others, so is God. I will always remember John 11 as the chapter when God cried. His tears came upon me unexpectedly, for I had never seen this side of Jesus before. But I must admit, I liked seeing it. Jesus was greatly troubled; He wept (John 11:35). Perhaps He wept because he felt compassion for the grief of His friends. This happens to me at funerals; I'm a social crier. It hits me hard when I see loved ones overcome with grief. Here, John uses the word "again" associated with Jesus' grief. John writes about His grief just a few verses prior (repetition makes me lean in): "Then Jesus, deeply moved again, came to the tomb" (John 11:38). And you know the rest of the story!

> Out of our brokenness, God creates.

Jesus had a strong bond with Lazarus, Mary, and Martha—as He wishes to have with you. God created a new life for Lazarus. Furthermore, He created belief for all who saw (and heard of) this miracle. In real time, they saw God's glory. God is still creating today through me, through you.

I like to give human qualities to inanimate objects. I wonder if the Potter apologizes to the pottery as He breaks it? Does He console it with His words? "This is going to hurt, dear one, but stay near to me; stay with the process." The Potter understands what being broken is all about. The Creator took my broken pieces and sealed me together with love and patience, like the kintsukuroi artist who carefully places gold lacquer in the cracks. I, too, feel the Creator's beautiful touch on my life.

Ann Voskamp, author of *The Broken Way*, writes, "Wounds can be openings to the beauty in us. And our weaknesses can be a container for God's glory." I am convinced that out of brokenness come beautiful things. Just as the finished piece of kintsukuroi is more beautiful than the original, so are you. Nature teaches us that the pearl in an oyster is made perfect by the stimulation of sand and grit in its shell. Take a lesson from nature: allow difficult circumstances to make you into something beautiful.

> That's when I call upon God to place a little more glory within. He has plenty. The whole Earth is filled with it.

After five years, the broken parts no longer cause agonizing pain. It can sting now and again, but that's when I call upon God to place a little more glory within. He has plenty. The whole Earth is filled with it.

Mary Oliver concludes her poem "The Summer Day" with a question. "Tell me, what it is you plan to do with your one wild and precious life?" Plan A didn't work out for me; I'm on to Plan B.

What am I going to do with this wild and precious new life of mine?

## A Call to Reinvent

In each stage of adulthood, we more or less reinvent ourselves. My eighteenth birthday brought its own state of euphoria. I traded my childhood lenses, the ones I shared with my parents, for new lenses—the lenses of adulthood, or so I thought. Ecstatic about my bright future, I fear it blinded others in my path. I soared along with wonder. Every day I conjured up new plans, some of which included attending Bible college, attending secular college, or being a nanny on the East Coast with a family I met in Sweden. When push came to shove, however, I decided not to stray too far from the nest; I stayed in Stockholm and worked as a nursing assistant. I quickly became attached to the patients, one in particular, a tiny bedridden lady, shrunken with age. Every possible chance, I sat with her. She loved my presence, and I loved hers.

Invariably our conversation turned to her garden—the one she'd never see again. Her descriptions evoked images from *The Secret Garden* where "every morning revealed new miracles." When an oxygen tank became her sole life support, it wasn't long before she passed from this life. She was wheeled out of the hospital, draped with a white cloth, followed by a grieving husband and son. I cleaned her room, sweeping every memory of her into my heart. I was taken aback by this first introduction to genuine sorrow and sadness. In retrospect, though, what a wonderful memory this beautiful soul imparted. After many years have passed, I love that her imagination still exists inside of me. Grief, both past and present, reminds us that life is precious and fleeting, and it serves to remind us that love never fails. Friends and family that pass from this life are extant within. Forever.

> **Grief, both past and present, reminds us that life is precious and fleeting.**

When I became a wife, I welcomed the chance to reinvent myself once again. Out of desire to learn more, I read books on marriage. I attended couple's retreats where I took copious notes. I easily settled into my new life doing those things my mother always did. Most days, I enjoyed homemaking. We lived on a college campus; I had finally settled on a career path, or so I thought, but this degree did not come to fruition. We decided to start a family. Thus, the mommy makeover began. My old lenses needed to be adjusted once again. Aiming high, I wanted to be the best mother, but my inadequacies surfaced. Research into motherhood began.

After my first son was born, I joined La Leche League International for mother-to-mother support that would give my infant the best start nutritionally. I read innumerable books on parenting. So focused, I rarely missed an episode of Focus on the Family. Another child came along. How ecstatic I was to be a mother of two boys. My own child-like sense of wonder returned. Looking through my sons' eyes, a spider web had great significance. It wasn't just a web of sticky residue to be destroyed with a broom—oh no—but strands of precious gold; a structure to be admired, one that would keep my oldest son entertained for hours. The backyard created all sorts of wonder for my two boys, as God's creation so aptly does. I've heard it said that children don't remember their best day of television, but they remember days in which they followed their curiosity and practiced creativity. Not wanting to part with my kids when they turned six, we made the decision to homeschool. Thus, the research began again. For the next twelve years, my role became teacher—it was reinvention of the best kind. I loved my role as homemaker, wife, mother, and teacher.

Now I'm on the other side. My kids are raised. My marriage has ended. Out of necessity, not desire, I am reinventing myself once again. I stepped away from the pain of divorce, dusted off the drawing board, and went to work. With the tool already in my hand—a desire to excel—I etched out a plan to create a new life full of happiness. I designed this new life out of my own desire and passion to create, like painters do on a canvas and writers do on a blank page. Entire worlds opened up to me. It's not too often in life where options are opened to us; they most often narrow. (Friends, please note: I am not glorifying divorce.) My sister Corinda helped me to see the unfolding of my new life with clarity. (We need these voices of reason and intellect in our lives.) *Career paths,*

**When I considered how happy I was at each stage in my life, it all came together for me; I could be happy again.**

*relationships, mortgages, bad habits, aging: they all have a way of limiting our options*, she said. These choices can limit our future. With the idea of the world being my oyster, I went to Barcelona to study Spanish; I went on a mission's trip to Scotland that lasted ten months; I moved to a different city. I now get to travel along new paths.

When I considered how happy I was at each stage in my life, it all came together for me; I could be happy again. I was confidant of this very thing. C.S. Lewis described how the idea for the story *The Lion, the Witch, and the Wardrobe* came to him in his teenage years. But it wasn't until he was forty that "Aslan came bounding into [the story]," and then the entire narrative came together for him. The idea came bounding into my story too: I was happy before; I will be happy again.

I have taken specific strides to find happiness in my new life. I always have something to look forward to now—whether it be a specialty coffee, an ice cream cone at Dairy Queen, or a trip. I endeavor to make my life sublime by following the lead of great people; I practice resilience.

## Always Have Something to Look Forward To

On the first day of spring, I awoke to a text from my niece inviting me to join her for ice cream. Dairy Queen offers free cones to celebrate the occasion. This started me thinking about Dairy Queen right off the bat. Several friends posted pictures of their cones on social media. (Social media has a way of making me dissatisfied with *all* the food in my fridge and cupboards.) I spent the morning fully anticipating an outing with my niece and great-nephews. Watching their eyes light up like it's Christmas morn as they ate their treat in celebration of spring was such a joy. Changing the course of my day with an unexpected treat of ice cream gave me something to look forward to.

I was impressed with Dairy Queen's sheer genius to get me thinking about ice cream so early in the morning. Their tweet that went out said, "Get your first taste of summer." I acquiesced.

Norman Vincent Peale said to "fill your mind with fresh, new creative thoughts of faith, love, and goodness. [And ice cream in this case.] By this process, you can actually remake your life." I endeavor to fill my mind with pleasant thoughts and dreams about my future. I look forward to seeing them come to fruition. My friend Colleen, speaks to children about praying their dreams. She admonishes them to turn their dreams into prayers. And

> **My dreams aligned with God's dreams for me; can it be?**

that's a sure-fire way to dream big. Happiness bubbles up inside when I turn my dreams into prayers. My dreams aligned with God's dreams for me; can it be?

If I was distracted from my pain by having something to look forward to on that spring morning, then I could use this same sort of energy to channel my wayward thoughts every day. The more I think about happiness, the happier I feel; research attests to this. I had to train my brain to think more productively. We could let someone else do it for us, like Dairy Queen, but I like the ideas Benjamin Franklin had on how to live a happier, more meaningful life as well.

## Make Your Life Sublime

Longfellow writes, "Lives of great men all remind us, we can make our lives sublime, and, departing, leave behind us, footprints on the sands of time." Benjamin Franklin was one of those people who left footprints on the sands of time. In an American literature course, we discussed him at length. One thing that captivated my interest was his plan for self-improvement. As I mentioned before, Franklin endeavored to practice thirteen virtues every day. For the sake of brevity, I will not list all of them. His thirteenth virtue, *Imitate Jesus and Socrates*, resonates with me the most. The first is a pretty tall order—perfection is impossible—but we certainly can strive to imitate Jesus. Daily, we can take steps to do this.

Franklin charted his efforts each evening as to how well he did with these virtues. We would do well to follow his lead—to chart our emotions and our happiness to see how well we are doing. Are you moving forward? Or do you need to go back and read Chapter 7 again? When I chart my happiness levels, I find that I'm happier more often than I am missing my former life. Benjamin Franklin established so many "firsts" for our country. We still enjoy the fruits of his creativity today.

Creating is a sure way to greater happiness. I desire to be more creative like my heavenly Father—the master Creator. (I might create something a little less grand, however!) God made us to be creative individuals. I know this because we are created in His image—in His creative nature. A tour of Ark Encounter in Williamstown, Kentucky, made me mindful of man's keen skill and profound creativity granted by God. Noah was given the instructions to build a massive ark, one without sails, without rudders. See, God wanted to direct the ship. Noah and his family were completely dependent upon God and the elements for direction, and for their final destination. Have you ever been there? The wind of the Spirit is pushing you along—to be like Him—to create. Noah's creativity provided a new life, one far more peaceful than the one he left behind. Six-hundred-year-old Noah began a new life. *There are always adjustments in life, Noah.* My ninety-three-year-old grandmother speaks to me yet again.

> Six-hundred-year-old Noah began a new life.

Whenever I think about creativity, I feel a stirring in my soul to create. To write. To paint. To bake. To draw.

I've recently joined an online class to learn the basics of drawing. Step-by-step tutorials on YouTube are fabulous and a great way to learn the fundamentals of drawing. It's those little tweaks and changes in my day that make me happier. My sister buys something every week from a foreign market to incorporate in her meals. Being a stay-at-home mom, she needs novelty. She's a neat lady, that sister of mine. If you'd like a unique prayer experience, pray while you create.

> **If you'd like a unique prayer experience, pray while you create.**

God "render[s] to a man according to his work" (Psalm 62:12). If I show up to write, God fills me with inspiration. Sometimes, I recognize God's voice amidst my own; other times, I recognize the voice of authors I've been reading. Sometimes, I only recognize my voice. I like to consider Ralph Waldo Emerson's words in his essay, Self-Reliance: "To believe your own thought, to believe that what is true for you in your private heart is true for all men" that he says, "is genius." I want to be careful not to "dismiss [my] thought because it is [mine]." I don't want moments of inspiration to pass me by because I believe my thoughts are subpar to the thoughts of others.

Like Noah, I am being pushed along too. Finally—it's about time—my whole being is moving forward. At one point, my flag and my sails were contrary. I've heard it said that in drawings or paintings, the ship's flag should be pointed in the direction that the ship is moving; the wind is pushing the ship forward through the waves. My efforts to move forward were thwarted by my mind's opposing forces. But when I linked my desires with God's desires, I felt this "pushing." Movement is good. My flags and sails adjusted themselves to match the direction in which the wind was blowing.

I was being pushed along partly by my own desire to create a new life, a happier one post-divorce. I visualize God's healing power pushing me along, like my father did for my mother while climbing a mountain in Liechtenstein. I'll never forget the visual of him placing his hand on her back and gently guiding her upward. In *The Power of Positive Thinking*, Norman Vincent Peale writes, "When you pray for something, at the same time visualize what you pray for. Believe that if it is God's will and is worthwhile, not selfishly sought after, but for human good, that it is at that moment given to you."

When moving forward, your whole being should be on board. You can't have an obstinate flag doing its own thing, pointing in the wrong direction. Here I am reminded of the sound of the mighty rushing wind in the 2nd chapter of Acts, the Holy Spirit. With the Spirit as my guide, I move forward "into all truth… and he will shew [me] things to come" (John 16:13, KJV). This is the Guide I want, pushing me along. He pushes us to be better, to be like Him.

Benjamin Franklin observed that "[m]any people live bad lives that would gladly live good ones, but do not

> **By making small daily improvements in his life, Franklin improved his happiness.**

know how to make the change." By making small daily improvements, Franklin improved his happiness. Franklin said, and I love these words, "On the whole, though I never arrived at the perfection I had been so ambitious of obtaining, but fell far short of it, yet I was, by the endeavor, a better and a happier man than I otherwise should have been if I had not attempted it." Although research shows that it takes ten thousand hours to become an expert at most things, we can start small, and take baby steps, thereby making daily improvements. What change can you make today to help you lead a healthier, more fulfilling life?

### Resilience

I know I've used this Scripture before, but I really do think about it often. It's resilience in just one Scripture. "Finally, brothers and sisters, whatever is true, whatever is noble, whatever is right, whatever is pure, whatever is lovely, whatever is admirable—if anything is excellent or praiseworthy—think about such things" (Philippians 4:8, NIV). This is how I define "such things": I become a tourist in my own city; I read beautiful books; I join a book club and a writer's group; I learn something new every day; I create daily.

Once I was able to "bear [my] own load" (Galatians 6:5), these are some of the things I did to find happiness.

*Be a tourist in my own city.* Go on field trips. Do you remember the excitement getting on the bus and going on a field trip in grade school? It's just as exciting today. And it really does help you to think about something else for a while. I got the idea of being a tourist in my own city from a travel literature course I took in college. Museums are wonderful places to spend a few hours with a friend, or alone, if you are so inclined.

Adventures await right outside my front door.

I have watched happy people; they become tourists in their own city. They don't travel far to find happiness; they find it right at home. It's an instant pick-me-up. Adventures await right outside my front door. On days when the divorce has me feeling out of sorts, a museum is the place for me. I especially enjoy the Impressionists' paintings. I am particularly drawn to Mary Cassatt's work. It is her story that makes me lean in.

Her parents moved the family to France (from the United States) for four years just because they thought it was a good idea, and they liked French culture. Agreed! Let's pack up and move to France.

When she grew up, Cassatt applied to an art school in Paris but was denied entrance because of her gender. Instead, she showed resilience by shaking off the

> # For Cassatt's resilience, I am a devotee.

disappointment. (My sister's advice to me is always the same: *shake it off!* It's good advice.) Cassatt became friends with artists like Degas, and other Impressionist and contemporary artists as well. The influence by the great artists can be seen in her work. For Cassatt's resilience, I am a devotee.

I love this quote by her: "There are two ways for a painter: the broad and easy one, or the narrow and hard one." Although I don't understand this quote in terms of painting, I can relate it to divorce. There is an easy path after divorce; there is a hard path. The easy path is where one doesn't grieve but jumps from relationship to relationship, looking for that feel-good emotion often mistaken for love. A relationship of this type is merely a bandage for a gaping wound; it covers the wound initially but does not bring healing. The hard way deals with pain head-on. You do the things I described in Chapter 5: attend divorce care classes, seek counseling, and devour books on healing. On that path, taking five years to heal, or longer if necessary, is okay. You take the necessary time to adjust to becoming single again. This advice applies to our relationship with God as well. My mother always says, "Serving God hard is easy, but serving God easy is hard." In the long run, the "easy" path is always the hardest one.

*Read beautiful books.* Children's literature has a way of lifting my spirit. I particularly love the *Secret*

*Garden* by Frances Hodgson Burnett, *Mandy* by Julie Andrews Edwards—she's an author too! Who knew? — and *Half Magic* by Edward Eager. Reading Laura Ingalls Wilder's *Little House* series as an adult brings back many wonderful childhood memories of reading these books. I love the memories I have of reading these to my sons as well.

*Join a book club. Join a writing group. Start one.* I'm in a writing group with friends. I meet with them monthly via conference call. They inspire me, and it is good to live inspired. I am currently in a book club and am the online facilitator with a group of friends for the book *Happier at Home* by Gretchen Rubin. If there isn't a group for what interests you, start one.

*Learn something new.* I went back to college where I learn something new daily (whether I want to or not!) Learning new ways to cook is a passion of mine. One of my favorite experiences was a cooking class in Rome. Even thinking about it makes me happy. At the hotel, I was given a map of Rome by the concierge. He traced the route I should take, and off I went. Trastevere was my destination and walking my only mode of transportation. The route took me past the ancient ruins of the Colosseum and the Forum, past the center of Rome, over the bridge of the Tiber River, and to one of the quaintest parts of Rome. After forty minutes of brisk walking, I found Via dei Fienaroli 5.

Introducing myself to Chef Andrea and the others, I immediately felt at home. Being a third culture kid, I thrive in such environments. Chef Andrea came highly recommended by TripAdvisor and after five minutes in his kitchen, I knew why! I learned that one should never cut basil, only tear it for best flavor. Garlic, after removing the heart, should be sautéed with the skin as well, not for flavor, but for health benefits. And deep-fried pumpkin blossoms stuffed with prosciutto and fresh mozzarella make a delicious appetizer.

I was apprehensive about going to this class alone in a foreign country. I'm glad I didn't allow my fears to dictate that day though. What a perfect experience it was!

### That New Thing

"Remember not the former things, nor consider the things of old. Behold I am doing a new thing" (Isaiah 43:18-19). How I wonder about those new things He is doing. And wondering is happiness, pure and simple.

In the National Portrait Gallery in Washington, D.C. hangs a life-size portrait of George Washington. You'd recognize it instantly, in a déjà vu sort of way. You've seen it before, many times, at church, at restaurants; you may even have an exact duplicate in your wallet but on a smaller scale. This same image—the head of the president—graces the dollar bill, only in reverse. Impressed with Gilbert Stuart's craft, there is so much to love about this painting, from the lace around his collar to his fancy shoes.

What struck me most, however, was the sky clearly visible through the picture window, the rainbow at the top

**Dark times give way to promising ones.**

right corner, and the less noticeable ominous clouds appearing directly opposite. In *Visual Intelligence*, Amy Herman writes, "[t]he rainbow was added to symbolize that America's first president had brought the young country through the storms of the previous decades and that prosperous days were ahead." Dark times give way to promising ones.

When I think back to the ending of my marriage, this analogy resonates. However, this is where I find myself now. The rain has stopped, the storm clouds abated. I've thrown wide the windows to my ark—I find it without rudders, without sails. The wind of the Spirit guided me on an angry sea safely through to today; it will continue to guide me. I look around. I am on the mountaintop with possibilities in every direction. There is nothing to look back to; it has been removed from my view. Oh, but I am not alone either. Those who loved me before all the chaos love me still, with all my imperfections.

Dark times have given way to promising times. It's a new day.

Hello new life.

# Coaching Corner

Dear Friend,

In times of trouble, we turn our lives over to God. He places His hands and fingerprints all over us. As with kintsukuroi, we are made stronger by His touch. He places people in our lives to help bear our burdens until we are able to "bear [our] own load" (Galatians 6:2-5). He returns our lives right back to us as if to say, "You've got this!" We can sit back and admire "what [God] has done as truly wonderful, wonderful proofs of his power beyond what any creature could perform" (Matthew Henry Commentary on Isaiah 25). I endeavor to admire what God is doing within; I admire the treasure that comes along with change.

Sometimes we don't see the treasure until the boat stops tossing along on the sea of change. What we thought was contrary wind was the very thing that got us to where we needed to be—atop the mountain. (Noah, remember?) With this in mind, endeavor to become what it is that God wants you to become. Becoming is done with patience, perseverance, and pure grit. Sometimes, we are hindered because we see we have so far to go to reach the mountaintop. The French philosopher, Voltaire, said, "The best is the enemy of the good." Don't be so concerned with perfection that you don't progress at all. We can be so focused on the "best" that we miss that which is good. Good is finding healing every day. The good thing to do here is to make daily improvements.

On his deathbed, Leonardo da Vinci apologized to the king of France, to God and as I see it, to humanity, for not "having worked at art as he should have." His struggle for perfection hindered his productivity. Georgio Vasari, author of *The Lives of the Artists,* writes of Leonardo, "[His] splendid and exceptional mind was hindered by the fact that he was too eager and that his constant search to add excellence to excellence and perfection to perfection was the reason why his work was slowed." Similarly, we can be immobilized by perfection, not moving ahead because we can't do it all right now. So, take baby steps instead. Consider this: how do you eat an elephant? One bite at a time.

God isn't looking for perfection—like Himself. He's looking for your best. (Your best might look different than my best. And today's best might look different than yesterday's best.) Yes, we are created in His image, but He didn't make us exactly like Him in His perfection. It's a good thing, too, because it is often in our imperfections, our mistakes, our times of brokenness that we bring out our best stories. And it is in those moments that the Creator goes back to the drawing board to help us create a new and wonderful life.

## *Prayer*

*Jesus, help me to accept change as it comes my way. I endeavor, above all, to be whole and healed. Help me to embrace being single again. Nostalgia's dark side keeps coming back to haunt me. I can no longer spend my energies on her fickle ways. Lord, help me delight in the process of healing and in becoming the person You wish me to be. Cause me to be thankful for this new life gifted to me, and let me see it as a gift. Each and every day help me to see Your new mercies. I am reminded in Scripture that Your "plans for [me] are too numerous to list" (Psalm 40:5, NLT). I pray that I will walk right into the plans You have for me. I pray that I may find all the good You have for me. Jesus, I fix my eyes on You, the founder and perfecter of my faith (Hebrews 12:2).*

## Your Turn

  ⬿ What is it about your new life that gives you hope?

  ⬿ How would the wisest person you know propel you to your new life?

  ⬿ How can you show gratitude for the treasures that adversity has gifted you?

❧ How will you adjust to being single again?

❧ What does it look like to be healed from divorce? Envision that. Write about it.

❧ How can you delight in this new season of your life?

❧ Are you immobilized by perfection? How can you do those things you know you must do—to heal, to thrive, to accept your new life?

❧ If you could watch God create you, what do you think He would place inside of you? How are you most like your Father?

❧ How are you, like kintsukuroi, more beautiful for having been broken?

❧ How do you recognize God's extraordinary work in your life?

# Acknowledgments

Corinda Woinarowicz's brilliance confounds me. Her feedback during this project has been crucial. Her thoughts carried my thoughts to where I intended them to go in the first place. An incredible communicator, she extracts the essence of an unfinished thought and polishes it to perfection. There aren't enough superlatives to describe Corinda's brilliance and flair. How blessed I am to call her sister and best friend.

Cori Smith, friend and trusted reader who always offers sage advice became my sounding board in Scotland and remains so to this day. Remnants of her are scattered throughout these pages. Her perspective is refreshing. One doesn't have to look long or hard to see her worth. She is a gift to all those around her, and one I treasure wholeheartedly.

My dad's keen eye and biblical knowledge is much appreciated. My mom is forever in my corner and my biggest fan. For their love and support, I am grateful.

My sons and daughter-in-love: my heart is called back to them again and again. They are home. When I am not with them, I want to be.

Dezzy Girl asked for the first copy of *Hello New Life* for her birthday. That touched me more than she'll ever know.

Thank you most of all to God. Without a doubt, His fingerprints are all over these pages. Left to myself, this book would have lacked inspiration.

# Resources

Clabaugh, Colleen. World Network of Prayer. wnop.org
Clemans, Carol. Christian Counseling. www.carolclemans.org.
Valley Christian Counseling, Fargo, ND.

*Books for Further Study*
Bertrand, Russell. *The Conquest of Happiness.* New York: H.
  Liveright, 1930.
Bevere, John. *The Bait of Satan: Living Free from the Deadly Trap of
  Offense.* Lake Mary: Charisma House, 1994.
Bloomfield, Harold, Melba Colgrove, and Peter McWillimas. *How to
  Survive the Loss of a Love.* Algonac: May Books/Prelude Press.
  1976.
Brown, Brené. *Braving the Wilderness: The Quest for True Belonging
  and the Courage to Stand Alone.* New York: Random House,
  2017.
Brown, Brené. *Daring Greatly: How the Courage to be Vulnerable
  Transforms the Way We Live, Love, Parent, and Lead.* New
  York: Avery, 2012.
Brown, Brené. *I Thought It Was Just Me (but it isn't): Making the
  Journey from "What Will People Think?" to "I Am Enough."*
  New York: Avery, 2007.
Brown, Brené. *Rising Strong: How the Ability to Reset Transforms
  the Way We Live, Love, Parent, and Lead.* New York: Spiegel &
  Grau, 2015.
Brown, Brené. *The Gifts of Imperfection: Let Go of Who You Think
  You're Supposed to Be and Embrace Who You Are.* Center City:
  Hazelden Publishing, 2010.
Cameron, Julia. *The Artist's Way: A Spiritual Path to Higher
  Creativity.* New York: Putnam Special Markets, 1992.
Cloud, Henry, and John Townsend. *Safe People: How to Find
  Relationships that Are Good for You and Avoid Those that
  Aren't.* Grand Rapids: Zondervan, 1996.
Cloud, Henry, and John Townsend. *When to Say Yes, When to Say No
  to Take Control of Your Life.* Grand Rapids: Zondervan, 1992.

David, Susan. *Emotional Agility: Get Unstuck, Embrace Change, and Thrive in Work and Life.* New York City: Avery, 2016.

Elliott, Susan J. *Getting Past Your Breakup: How to Turn a Devastating Loss into the Best Thing that Ever Happened to You.* Cambridge:Da Capo Press, 2009.

Fisher, Bruce, and Robert Albert. *Rebuilding When Your Relationship Ends.* Atascadero: Impact Publishers, 1981.

Foster, Richard J. *Sanctuary of the Soul: Journey into Meditative Prayer.* London: Inter-Varsity Press, 2011.

Gire, Ken. *Windows of the Soul: Hearing God in the Everyday Moments of Your Life.* Grand Rapids: Zondervan, 1996.

Greitens, Eric. *Resilience: Hard-Won Wisdom for Living a Better Life.* New York: Houghton Mifflin Harcourt Publishing, 2015.

Gurley, Ken. *The Point of Low Points.* Hazelwood: Word Aflame Press, 2013.

Herman, Amy. *Visual Intelligence: Sharpen Your Perception, Change Your Life.* New York: Houghton Mifflin Harcourt, 2016.

Holiday, Ryan. *The Obstacle is the Way: The Timeless Art of Turning Trials into Triumph.* New York: Penguin Group, 2014.

Johnson, Spencer. *Who Moved My Cheese?: An Amazing Way to Deal with Change in Your Work and in Your Life.* New York: G.P. Putnam's Sons Publishers, 1998.

Johnson, Spencer. *Peaks and Valleys: Making Good and Bad Times Work for You at Work and In Life.* New York: Atria Books, 2009.

Klein, Charles. *How to Forgive When You Can't Forget.* New York: Berkley Publishing, 1995.

Kushner, Harold S. *When Bad Things Happen to Good People.* Reprint ed. New York: Anchor, 2004.

Lewis, C.S. *A Grief Observed.* United Kingdom: Faber and Faber, 1961.

Lucado, Max. *Grace: More Than We Deserve, Greater Than We Imagine.* Nashville: Thomas Nelson, 2014.

Lucado, Max. *You'll Get Through This: Hope and Help for Your Turbulent Times.* Nashville:Thomas Nelson, 2015.

Marques, Joan. *101 Pebbles To Pave Your Way Through the Day.* Burbank: House of Metta, 2012.

Maxwell, John C. *How Successful People Grow: 15 Ways to Get Ahead in Life.* New York: Center Street, 2014

Maxwell, John C. *Intentional Living: Choosing a Life That Matters.* New York: Center Street, 2015.

Maxwell, John C. *Sometime You Win Sometimes You Learn: Life's Greatest Lessons Are Gained from Our Losses.* New York: Center Street, 2013.

Niequist, Shauna. *Present Over Perfect: Leaving Behind Frantic for a Simpler, More Soulful Way of Living.* Grand Rapids: Zondervan, 2016.

Nouwen, Henri. *The Inner Voice of Love: A Journey Through Anguish to Freedom.* New York: Double Day, 1996.

Peale, Norman Vincent. *The Power of Positive Thinking.* New York: Simon & Schuster, 1952.

Roig-DeBellis, Kaitlin. *Moving Forward from Life's Darkest Hours.* New York: G.P. Putnam Sons Publishers, 2015.

Rubin, Gretchen. *Better Than Before: Mastering the Habits of Our Everyday Lives.* New York: Crown Publishers, 2015.

Rubin, Gretchen. *Happier at Home: Kiss More, Jump More, Abandon Self-Control, and My Other Experiments in Everyday Life.* New York: Crown Publishers, 2012.

Rubin, Gretchen. *The Happiness Project: Or, Why I Spent a Year Trying to Sing in the Morning, Clean my Closets, Fight Right, Read Aristotle, and Generally Have More Fun.* New York: HarperCollins, 2009.

TerKeurst, Lysa. *Uninvited: Living Loved When You Feel Less Than, Left Out, and Lonely.* Nashville: Thomas Nelson, 2016.

Tutu, Desomond, and Mpho Tutu. Reprint Ed. *The Book of Forgiving: The Fourfold Path of Forgiving Ourselves and Our World.* New York: HarperCollins, 2014.

Voskamp, Ann. *The Broken Way: A Daring Path into the Abundant Life.* Grand Rapids: Zondervan, 2016.

Warren, Kay. *Choose Joy: Because Happiness Isn't Enough.* Grand Rapids: Revell, 2012.

Warren, Rick. *The Purpose Driven Life: What on Earth Am I Here For?* Grand Rapids: Zondervan, 2001.

Wright, H. Norman. Ebook ed. *A Better Way to Think: How Positive Thoughts Can Change Your Life.* Grand Rapids: Revell, 2011.

# Bibliography

## 1

Elliott, Susan J. *Getting Past Your Breakup: How to Turn a Devastating Loss into the Best Thing that Ever Happened to You.* Cambridge: Da Capo Press, 2009.

Heap, Kris. "Amazing Advice on Happiness at 92-years Old." Successify. 10 April 2014.

Lewis, C.S. *A Grief Observed.* United Kingdom: Faber and Faber, 1961.

Messenger, Stephen. "How One Genius Little Fish Convinces Sharks Not to Eat Them." *www.thedodo.com. 14 August 2014. https://www.thedodo.com/how-one-genius-little-fish-con-672797576.html. Accessed 22 March 2017.*

Peale, Norman Vincent. *The Power of Positive Thinking.* New York: Simon & Schuster, 1952.

Twain, Mark. *The Adventures of Huckleberry Finn.* New York: Bantam Books, 1981.

## 2

Austen, Jane. *Pride and Prejudice.* Edited by James Kinsley. New York: Oxford University Press, 2004.

Brown, Brené. *Daring Greatly: How the Courage to Be Vulnerable Transforms the Way We Live, Love, Parent, and Lead.* New York City: Avery, 2012. Print.

Brown, Brené. *The Gifts of Imperfection: Let Go of Who You Think You're Supposed to Be and Embrace Who You Are.* Center City, Hazelden Publishing, 2010.

Carroll, Lewis. *Alice in Wonderland and Through the Looking Glass.* Grosset & Dunlap, Publishers, 1946.

Cloud, Henry, and John Townsend. *Safe People: How to Find Relationships that Are Good for You and Avoid Those that Aren't.* Grand Rapids: Zondervan, 1996.

Cowman, L.B, and James Reimann. *Streams in the Desert.* Revised
ed. Grand Rapids: Zondervan, 1999.

David, Susan. *Emotional Agility: Get Unstuck, Embrace Change, and
Thrive in Work and Life.* New York City: Avery, 2016. Print.

Elliott, Susan. *Getting Past Your Breakup: How to Turn a
Devastating Loss into the Best Thing that Ever Happened to You.*
Cambridge: DaCapo Press, 2009. Print.

Frankl, Victor. *Man's Search for Meaning.* 3rd ed. New York City:
Touchstone, 1984. Print.

Johnson, Spencer. *Who Moved My Cheese?: An Amazing Way to
Deal with Change in Your Work and in Your Life.* New York:
G.P. Putnam's Sons Publishers, 1998.

Littles, James. "Don't Waste the Bread or the Storms." The
Sanctuary, a United Pentecostal Church. 26 November 2017.
Sermon, November 26, 2017. http://www.thesanctuaryupc.com

Shakespeare, William. 1564-1616. *The Tempest.* New York: Simon
and Schuster, 1994.

*Word Aflame Apostolic Study Bible.* Edited by Robin Johnston.
"Ecclesiastes." Hazelwood: Word Aflame Press, 2014.

### 3

Barnes, Albert. Heritage Ed. "Psalms." Barnes Book Notes. Grand
Rapids: Baker Books, Reprinted 1996.

Dickens, Charles. *A Tale of Two Cities, and Great Expectations.*
Diamond ed. Ticknor and Fields, 1867.

Henry, Matthew. (1662-1714). "I Kings." "Joshua." *Matthew Henry's
Concise Commentary on the Whole Bible.* Nashville: Thomas
Nelson, Reprinted 1997.

Hunt, William Holman. *The Light of the World.* 1853, oil on canvas,
St. Paul's Cathedral, London.

Le Billon, Karen. *French Kids Eat Everything: How Our Family Moved to France, Cured Picky Eating, Banned Snacking, and Discovered 10 Simple Rules for Happy, Healthy Eaters.* New York: HarperCollins, 2012.

Roethke, Theodore. "In a Dark Time." *The Collected Poems of Theodore Roethke.* University of Washington Press, 1982.

Spurgeon, C.H. *Morning and Evening: King James Version/ A Devotional Classic For Daily Encouragement.* Peabody: Hendrickson Publisher, 1991.

Strong, James. *The New Strong's Expanded Exhaustive Concordance of the Bible.* Nashville: Thomas Nelson, 2010.


### 4

Fisher, Dennis. "All Through This Hour." *Our Daily Bread.* September 2013. https://odb.org/2013/09/09/all-through-this-hour. Accessed 10 May 2017.

Gire, Ken. *Windows of the Soul: Hearing God in the Everyday Moments of Your Life.* Grand Rapids: Zondervan, 1996.

Henry, Matthew. (1662-1714). "John." *Matthew Henry's Concise Commentary on the Whole Bible.* Nashville: Thomas Nelson, Reprinted 1997.

Miller, Bryan. "Eating out: With Luciano Pavarotti; For Pavarotti, the Proof's in the Pasta." October 1988. www.nytimes.com/1988/1john 0/19/garden/eating-out-with-luciano-pavarotti-for-pavarotti-the-proof-s-in-the-pasta.html. Accessed 15 October 2017.

Rubin, Gretchen. *The Four Tendencies: The Indispensible Personality Profiles That Reveal How to Make Your Life Better (and Other People's Lives Better, Too).* New York: Penguin Random House, 2017.

Wagner, Lori. "Wisdom Is a Lady: Using Godly Wisdom to Build a Life of Purpose." Hazelwood: Word Aflame Press, 2014. Presentation.

## 5

Bloomfield, Harold, Melba Colgrove, and Peter McWillimas. *How to Survive the Loss of a Love.* Algonac: May Books/Prelude Press. 1976.

Brown, Brené. *Daring Greatly: How the Courage to be Vulnerable Transforms the Way We Live, Love, Parent, and Lead.* New York: Avery, 2012.

Elliott, Susan J. *Getting Past Your Breakup: How to Turn a Devastating Loss into the Best Thing that Ever Happened to You.* Cambridge:Da Capo Press, 2009.

Fisher, Bruce, and Robert Albert. *Rebuilding When Your Relationship Ends.* Atascadero: Impact Publishers, 1981.

Pelley, S. (2017). *Fighting Famine in War-torn South Sudan.* cbsnews.com/. Retrieved from http://www.cbsnews.com/news/fighting-south-sudan-famine/

Greitens, Eric. *Resilience: Hard-Won Wisdom for Living a Better Life.* New York: Houghton Mifflin Harcourt Publishing, 2015.

Nouwen, Henri. *The Inner Voice of Love: A Journey Through Anguish to Freedom.* New York: Double Day, 1996.

Teresa of Ávila. (1515-1582). "Christ Has No Body."

Warren, Kay. *Choose Joy: Because Happiness Isn't Enough.* Grand Rapids: Revell, 2012.

Shakespeare, William. 1564-1616. *Macbeth.* New York: Simon &Schuster, 2013.

## 6

Da Vinci, Leonardo. *The Last Supper.* 1494-1498, oil/tempera on wall. Santa Maria delle Grazie, Milan.

Henry, Matthew. (1662-1714). "Genesis." *Matthew Henry's Concise Commentary on the Whole Bible.* Nashville: Thomas Nelson, Reprinted 1997.

Klein, Charles. *How to Forgive When You Can't Forget: Healing Our Personal Relationships.* Bellmore: Liebling Press, 1995.

Lewis, C.S. *Mere Christianity.* London: Macmillan, 1977.

Peale, Norman Vincent. *The Power of Positive Thinking.* New York: Simon & Schuster, 1952.

Smedes, Lewis. *Forgive & Forget: Healing the Hurts We Don't Deserve.* 2nd Ed. San Francisco:HarperOne, 2007.

Tutu, Desomond and Mpho Tutu. Reprint Ed. *The Book of Forgiving: The Fourfold Path of Forgiving Ourselves and Our World.* New York: HarperCollins, 2014.

*Word Aflame Apostolic Study Bible.* Edited by Robin Johnston. "Acts." Hazelwood: Word Aflame Press, 2014.

7

Brown, Brené. *Daring Greatly: How the Courage to be Vulnerable Transforms the Way We Live, Love, Parent, and Lead.* New York: Avery, 2012.

Connor, Steve. "Scientists prove it really is a thin line between love and hate." Independent. 29 October 2008. Retrieved from http://www.independent.co.uk/news/science/scientists-prove-it-really-is-a-thin-line-between-love-and-hate-976901.html

Cameron, Julia. *The Artist's Way: A Spiritual Path to Higher Creativity.* New York: Putnam Special Markets, 1992.

David, Susan. *Emotional Agility: Get Unstuck, Embrace Change, and Thrive in Work and Life.* New York City: Avery, 2016. Print.

Franklin, Benjamin. *The Autobiography of Benjamin Franklin.* Edited by Stanley Applebaum and Philip Smith. Philadelphia: Dover Publications, 1996.

Griggs. Mary B. "Medieval Knights on a Treadmill Put Historical Myths to the Test." Popular Mechanics. 21 July 2011. Web.

"Hernán Cortés." Biography.com. https://www.biography.com/people/hernán-cortés-9258320. Date accessed: August 26, 2017.

Lamott, Anne. "12 Truths I Learned from Life and Writing." TED. June 2017. Lecture.

MacLaren, Alexander (1826-1919). "Ephesians." *MacLaren's Commentary: Expositions of the Holy Scripture.* Harrington: Delmarva Publications, 2013.

Nkrumah, Kwame. "Forward Ever." Speech. 24 October 1954.

Nouwen, Henri. *The Inner Voice of Love: A Journey Through Anguish to Freedom.* New York: Double Day, 1996.

Robinson, Marilyn. *Gilead: A Novel.* New York: Picador, 2004.

Roig-DeBellis, Kaitlin. *Moving Forward from Life's Darkest Hours.* New York: G.P. Putnam Sons Publishers, 2015.

Roosevelt, Theodore. "Citizenship in a Republic" and/or "The Man in the Arena." Speech Delivered at the Sorbonne. Paris, France, 1910.

Spence, Henry D. M. "Ephesians." *The Complete Pulpit Commentary.* Harrington: Delmarva, 2013.

Service, Robert William. "The Call of the Wild." The Spell of the Yukon and Other Verses. New York: Barse & Hopkins, 1907.

Solomon, Deborah. "The Priest: Questions for Archbishop Desmond Tutu." *The New York Times Magazine.* 4 March 2010.

*Word Aflame Apostolic Study Bible.* Edited by Robin Johnston. "Ephesians." *Word Aflame Apostolic Study Bible.* Hazelwood: Word Aflame Press, 2014.

Wright, H. Norman. eBook ed. *A Better Way to Think: How Positive Thoughts Can Change Your Life.* Grand Rapids: Revell, 2011.

**8**

Alluvia, Richard. "The Chronicles of Narnia: The Lion, the Witch, and the Wardrobe." *Commonweal.* 2006. https://www.commonwealmagazine.org/chronicles-narnia-lion-witch-and-wardrobe

Burnett, Frances Hodgson. *The Secret Garden.* New York: HarperCollins, 1911.

Doyle, John Sean. "Resilience, Growth & Kintsukuroi." *Psychology Today.* 3 October 2015. Date accessed 5 September 2017.

Emerson, Ralph Waldo. "Self-Reliance." Collected Essays, 1841.

Franklin, Benjamin. *The Autobiography of Benjamin Franklin.* London: J. Parsons, 1793

Havemeyer, Louisiana. "On Mary Cassatt." *Explore PAHistory.com.* Date accessed 22 November 2017.

Henry, Matthew. (1662-1714). "Isaiah." *Matthew Henry's Concise Commentary on the Whole Bible.* Nashville: Thomas Nelson, Reprinted 1997.

Herman, Amy. *Visual Intelligence: Sharpen Your Perception, Change Your Life.* New York: Houghton Mifflin Harcourt, 2016.

Longfellow, Henry Wadsworth. "A Psalm of Life." Selected Poems. 1838.

Oliver, Mary. "The Summer Day." *New and Selected Poems.* Boston: Beacon Press, 1992

Peale, Norman Vincent. *The Power of Positive Thinking.* New York: Simon & Schuster, 1952.

Rubin, Gretchen. *Happier at Home: Kiss More, Jump More, Abondon Self-Control, and My Other Experiments in Everyday Life.* New York: Crown Publishers, 2012.

Stryk, Lucien, and Takashi Ikemoto. *Zen Poetry: Let the Spring Breeze Enter.* Grove Press, 1995.

Stuart, Gilbert. *Lansdowne Portrait.* 1796, oil on canvas, National Portrait Gallery. Washington, D.C.

Vasari, Giorgio (1511-1574). Reissue ed. *The Lives of the Artists.* Translated and Introduction by Julia Conway and Peter Bondanella. New York: Oxford University Press, 2008.

Voskamp, Ann. *The Broken Way: A Daring Path into the Abundant Life.* Grand Rapids: Zondervan, 2016.

88608002R00083

Made in the USA
Lexington, KY
14 May 2018